HOW TO BECOME A DIGITAL MARKETING HERO

Rufus Lidman

Clink
Street

London | New York

Script Editor: Malin Johansson
Translated by: Sebastian Prochéus

Published by Clink Street Publishing 2018

ISBNs:
978-1-912562-21-3 paperback
978-1-912562-22-0 ebook

CONTENTS

THE DIGITAL FOREWORD

You have just flipped open the first page of the book that is about to turn you into a digital hero. If you're already doing pretty well, you will become an expert. If you're already an expert, you will hone yourself to perfection and turn yourself into a structured digital guru with an even higher rate of success than before. And if you have never even heard of digital marketing and sales before, this book will offer good insight into the absolutely hottest topic of the modern day, and one of few topics that is all but guaranteed to be just as important tomorrow as it is today.

What can't be guaranteed however, is that the data in the book is up to date. The pace at which digital marketing and sales (DMS) is moving is breathtaking. Anyone trying to maintain some sort of outpost at the forefront of this subject is pretty much "repairing an airplane in flight". Even when you are holding this in your hand, some of the data provided probably already past its expiry date, much in the same way that some of the tactical details may have changed from the point they were written down, to the point when you read them. That having been said, the methods and tools we will soon delve into, are together nothing short of a highway to the very cutting edge of DMS—and hopefully beyond.

But the dynamic nature of this field is also what makes

it so very exciting for those who thrive on thrills. For that reason, this book does not seek to give you the "latest" of digital data. Insteadit will give you a strategic platform and the tools you need to perform digital miracles.

But who am I to promise you these shiny things? What reason do you have to believe all these bold words of mine? Well, above all else, I guess the decade of digital adventures and success stories—both my own and others—might be a start. So, in the spirit of credibility, here is a rundown of my digital past:

I started my first company as a 19-year-old teenager, and ever since the rise of the digital I have performed innumerable audits and due diligences, founded and actively engineered some ten digital entrepreneur companies, raised capital in half a dozen more, experienced attractive exits, and been part of boards of directors both at startups and on the stock exchange.I have developed hundreds of digital strategies and digital sanity checks for several billion-dollar companies in Stockholm, London, Barcelona, New York, Seoul and Singapore—just to name a few. I aided in the founding of the Interactive Advertising Bureau (IAB), and was honored to be elected digital advisor for the world's biggest marketing organization (The Swedish part of WFA, The world Federation of Advertisors, representing as much as 90% of the media investments in the world). During this time, I have worked with some of the world's biggest companies in the fields of home electronics, household appliances, computer software, electricity, interior design, auditing, automobiles, financing, dating and gaming. Again, just to name a few.

But I suppose I'm most known (so far) for having published one of the very first books on digital strategy, held hundreds of lectures for tens of thousands of people, and hosted one of most visited blogs in the field. But, most recent and most important of all, 2017 I launched DMP, the worlds' 2nd

most downloaded application within DMS, built on a similar base as this book but with microlearning format. Three months since launch the app had more than 100.000 installs, with most impressing speed in Asia from markets like India, Vietnam, Indonesia and South Korea, but also huge explosion in Latin America and intense downloads form USA, UK and english speaking Africa. Today it has more than 150.000 users and intensively moving up, it is the highest ranked in reviews for DMS in the world – ahead of Philip Kotler and now only Google ahead of us. In search it is ranked nr 1 in Appstore and Google Play at all giant markets such like India, USA and Brazil, before giants such as Udemy, Linkedin and even before Google itself.

Still my message here is not *look at all the cool things I've done.* My point is that I have been doing this on an intense level for the better part of my life, and I know what this field requires of the ambitious marketer. I know where the pitfalls are. I know the ins and outs, the risks, the secrets.With that kind of background, it would be a strange thing indeed if I had not accumulated at least some experience. I have seen major companies take their old analog processes and technology and transform them into something digital, hoping it will magically make them more appealing. I have also seen small, insignificant South-East Asian companies completely nail their digital transformations, using minimal budgets to launch extremely successful SMM campaigns with flyers and billboards outside important high schools.

I have seen people struggle so much with their digital programs that they have effectively tied themselves into knots with internal marketing in their pursuit of more ROI:al external marketing. I have seen antiquated IT consultants launch digital $10 and $100-million projects; and I have seen them crash and burn, thanks to drawn-out procedures that have seen the technology grow obsolete even before launch. I have seen the coolest intrapreneurs wage futile wars on internal silos and ear-marked budgets. I have seen how advertisers who have finally opened their eyes and wallets have to actually educate external agencies still stuck in the ancient, pre*net*al world. When that has worked, I have beheld inspiring triumphs... and when it hasn't, I have witnessed great failures. And I have also seen how companies that have had the wisdom to learn from their mistakes have proceeded to remodel their enterprises into digital masterpieces for the ages.

All in all, I have experienced a whole lot, and amid all these experiences there has always been a common denominator: the value of a digital strategy that helps guide the way to our goals using the least amount of resources in the shortest possible time. As a matter of fact, it is from the collected arsenal of all these impressions that this book has finally come to life. In the chapters to follow we will structure, analyze and systematically treat them, and then, seasoned in a goodly helping of big data and meta-studies, reflect on their meaning.

Bon appétit.

CHAPTER 1:
THE DIGITAL TSUNAMI

What will we learn? *How the whole world is going from offline to online.*
Why is this important? *To understand the consequences for companies and teams.*

Over the last couple of years, marketers have been completely flooded by a digital tsunami. With several billion people across the globe connected to a collective network, the digital media consumption is completely out of this world. This has entailed big consequences for societies all over the world, for companies and individuals alike. For many countries, this digital blitz-expansion has become a crucial GDP growth component.

For companies and lone marketers, the development has been equally steep. In just shy of a decade, the prevalence of digital marketing has undergone a remarkable expansion, and the digitalization crusade is expected to keep growing just as epidemically in the coming years. However, international studies show that a surprisingly low number of marketers are confident that their digital campaigns will even work. In other words, while the explosive evolution of digital media consumption has goaded us marketers into opening our wallets, we still don't really know how to realize the true potential of our campaigns. This book seeks to close that gap.

In this chapter we will take a look at how the digital tsunami has flushed across every company worth its name. We will learn how the entire world is shedding the material bonds of the offline world and uploading itself to the web. We will see how dramatic the increase in consumers' media consumption really is, and just how vital the role of digital marketing is and will continue to be in the modern marketer's life.

Please wait... uploading the world

The entire world is in the process of going from offline to online. The number of internet users has increased with around 1500% since the turn of the millennium—today there are soon 4 billion people surfing the World Wide Web. There are more mobile devices than there are actual people, and we're not just talking quantity when it comes to connectivity—the quality has become significantly better too. More than 80% of the global population has access to 3G network and around 50% to 4G.

This digital tsunami, which has flushed across our world, has left traces everywhere. The digital has grown to become truly vital to the overall health of countries. Some of the world's most digitalized countries have extraordinary internet penetration, such as Norway (98%), Denmark (96%) and Iceland (100%). With such numbers, it is not exactly a mystery why countries' health can hinge on its population's online and digital behavior.

INTERNET USE
(in millions)

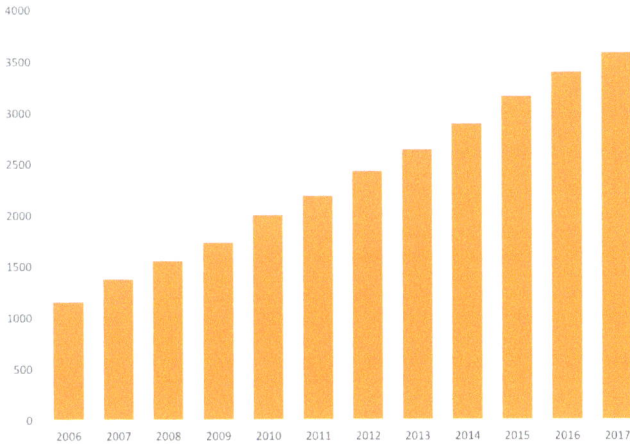

Marketers with a worthy cause

Naturally, these national statistics are not solely derived from "digital marketing". Adding to that number are things like e/m-commerce, email usage, mobile phones and all kinds of media consumption, as well as other aspects of digital *information, interaction* and *transactions*. What it does indicate though, is that all of us who work with digital marketing and sales are doing something highly relevant and important, and unlike many traditional markets, ours is not only being torn to shreds by a disruptive paradigm shift—it is in fact complicit in causing it.

And as people's wallets swell, that has only become all the more evident. Just after the Millennium Shift, digital marketing composed 3% of the total marketing pie in one of my two home countries Sweden. I was one of few who claimed that those 3% would grow to 10% in less than ten years. This was just after the big IT crash, and my audience laughed to

7

the point where they would have thrown tomatoes at me, if only they had brought any.

But they were wrong. And actually, so was I—10% turned out to be entirely off target; it ended up being 20%. In my previous book from 2011, I maintained that it would reach 30% before 2014 (which happened). Today, just a few years later, that number is approaching 50%, and I daresay that within five years, it will be well over 80%—let's see if anyone's laughing this time.

And if these things are not enough to convince you of how important the digital is, here are some more mind-boggling statistics. At the time of writing, there are 270 billion sent emails; 1 billion hours of watched YouTube video; over 10 billion video views on Snapchat; 5 billion likes; 6.5 billion searches; 1.6 billion Tinder swipes; 500 million tweets. *Every day.* All of this is going on in channels where digital dialog and personalization are so very essential concepts. Meanwhile advertisers and agencies place next to every cent on their beloved traditional monologs… just like we used to do back in the prenetal days. We took print ads, TVCs and catalog texts from the Yellow Pages, rebranded them banners, video banners and Google ads, and uploaded them to the internet in the pale hope that somehow they would become sexier just because they were online.

I think most people realize that the expiry date for such digital investments is long past due. Or, in more strategic terms: it is time to stop using new technology to repair old processes, and instead use them to innovate new ones. Of the two, which one do you think creates the leaders of tomorrow? And while we're guessing: which one do you think is the prime reason only 9% of international marketers actually feel confident that their digital campaigns will yield the intended effect?

A threefold game plan

Since we are not interested in getting stuck in yesterday's solutions to tomorrow's problems, we will in this book adhere to three primary principles:

1. *Genuine strategy—prioritization and choice of path*
   In this book, we will only engage in *genuine* strategy— that is, *not* the tactical or operative aspects of how companies solve their practical everyday challenges, but the prioritization and strategic choices of path that decide what they will focus on, invest in, and later also which partners and systems will be important for them.

   This will make it clear what specifically employees should be educated in, even at high level. Our goal is to create and manage a flexible and strategic framework, but it will be different for every company. Everyone's goals, target audiences, resources, context, market and specific challenges differ. Experience has proven that an elastic strategic framework is easy to revise and supplement with new content according to the numerous changes occurring in both the world at large and each company's respective industry.

2. *Assessing the winds of the digital world*
   Our second ambition is that the team responsible for the considerable accumulation of digital marketing knowledge, established theory and big data research that lies at the heart of this book, will keep doing the very same job on an annual basis and subsequently publish the results.

   The idea is to not only update the data, but also perform thorough trendspotting on a global scale to assess how the digital winds are blowing; to elucidate potential ramifications for societies, industries or specific target audiences; to analyze how the corporate worlds evolve;

and, perhaps most importantly, to keep up with the avant-garde evolution of DMS. The digital ecosystem is a living and mercurial thing, and its various components will keep changing character. The importance of its various functions will fluctuate. Some will fall away completely even as others are brought into the fold, as we steadily progress from digital silos to a single omnipotent omnichannel.

This major review of the digital world will be done once a year and will be presented as a thorough Digital Trendspotting (keep your eyes peeled at www.aiar.com/academy).

3. *Supplementary information online*
   Our third ambition is perhaps the most contemporaneously important and relevant. Knowledge in DMS is fundamentally different from knowledge in e.g. mathematics and history—in fact, different from most professional educations. The industry is moving with such blazing speed that what I lecture about one month is completely out of date the next. Because of this, even a frequently updated book filled with the absolutely latest in DMS would not be able to fill the practical need a modern-day marketer with modern-day challenges has.

   To address this issue of a subject field that is constantly morphing, and so rapidly at that, the team behind the data accumulation of this book has released the first in a series of digital marketing applications designed to be both readily accessible to people, and easy to update with the latest in DMS. The applications rely on the cutting-edge microlearning concept and presents knowledge as compact, easily digestible nuggets that can be consumed anytime, anywhere and by anyone. The applications rely on an innovative 3T method that teaches readers the ropes in *Tutorials*;

certifies their knowledge in *Tests*; and then allows them to apply it on a practical level in *Tools*. The flagship application in this series—*Digital Marketing Pro*—is available in both AppStore and Google Play. You can read more about it on www.aiar.com.

The digital disposition

The book consists of seven chapters which are divided into four blocks: the digital warmup, the digital strategy, the digital context and the digital future. To some extent, these blocks can each be read separately as a sort of "practical manual" for the different subjects they each cover. If you're looking to become a master of the art of DMS though, you are strongly advised to read the book from start to finish to get a more comprehensive understanding of digital strategy. While the five first chapters are educational on a highly strategic and technical level, the final two chapters are more inspiring and instructional inquiries into the digital revolution at play in the world.

The first block—which we're already halfway through—is an introductory warmup session with a take-off point in the central goings-on of the world.

The next block consists of Chapters 2–3 and comprises what could very well be called the heart of the book. These two chapters ought to be read one right after the other and should not be skipped by anyone.

In **Chapter 2** we will learn more about the five most valuable tools in the arsenal of the digital marketer: social media, display, search, site and digital CRM. Each means is clearly defined and illustrated with examples, and we take a look at their prevalence and significance. The chapter also delineates certain moderating variables that are important to keep in mind. Finally, each means' pros and cons are presented in terms of *effect* vs *investment*.

In **Chapter 3** we dive deep into a tried-and-true 7-step process specifically designed for the development of a digital strategy that has the greatest likelihood of reaching its goals, with the least amount of resources in the shortest possible time. A wide array of steps will be treated: we will analyze background materials, perform goals and means analyses, perform an optimal matching of the means and goals, compare and specify economic and HR resources, find synergies and redundancies with other strategies, and outline an activity plans with goals and subgoals.

By absorbing the lessons of the second block, we will have a very firm foundation for our digital strategy or, at least as important, nurturing a more "strategic mindset" within DMS. As previously mentioned, these two chapters are the heart and soul of the book, but the following two will grant a 360-degree perspective of what it is like to not only work in an organization whose ambition it is to stay relevant in an increasingly more digital present, but perhaps even lead one. This is treated in the third block, the digital context, which connects external strategy with internal organization, using objective metrics as glue.

In **Chapter 4** we will take a close look at the immensely valuable possibilities for optimization as made available by digital analysis. The myth of the complexity of digital analysis is debunked, and the chapter then proceeds to explain how data derived from digital audits is the most reliable there is, and how extremely easy they are to perform and properly manage. We will focus specifically on digital key performance indicators (KPIs), how they are identified for each individual company, and how they are easily specified using a simple 4-step process and a 3-dimensional reference sheet.

In **Chapter 5** we will initially go over the reasons behind the digital paradigm shift—from disruptive communication technology to freedom-hungry consumers and digital commercialization. Above all else though, the chapter substantializes the revolutionizing effects the digital transformation has on societies, industries, companies and individual people. In more specific terms, we will see what effects the disruptive technology has on traditional industries; what the consequences for both the increasingly more digital communication and elastic organizations are; and how the changes in competency requirements and lifelong learning via digitallearning affect individual people.

After finishing Chapters 3 and 4 we will not only have built a sturdy foundation for the creation of a successful digital strategy, but also pieced it together with two additional prerequisites for digital success—digital analysis and the digital organization.

These are vital premises for becoming a digital hero today. But what is needed to remain a digital hero *tomorrow*? This is what the fourth and final block addresses—the digital future.

In **Chapter 6** we will perform a highlevel trendspotting of what is going on in the digital world, and then explore what repercussions this will have on digital marketing and sales. These trends include such things as record-high digital business; digital social relations as a next evolutionary step after traditional interaction; video media and interactive content as the undisputed champion over the static counterparts; and digital data as the mastermind behind everything.

In **Chapter 7** we will take a look at the conscious machines of tomorrow, i.e. bots. We will discuss the functions, possibilities and consequences these bots will have, and then finish with a personal e-pilog. All in the spirit of "if you haven't understood this, you haven't understood anything".

To whom it may concern

So, who is this book for? Who exactly are we helping sort out their digital activities? Who is so privileged that they will be part of tomorrow's most efficient digitalists and *real* winners? Who will these digital heroes be?

For those of the most practical minds, the question becomes: who should develop a company's digital strategy? The obvious answer is that the marketer himself should do it, and if not together with an independent third party, then entirely by himself. *Anything* but an agency, system provider or IT consultant… unless you want a strategy that is formulated to allocate as much budget and assignments as possible to the agency, system provider or IT consultant.

For those of somewhat broader perspectives though, it is a question of infinitely larger proportions. It's about all those who are affected by the digital's many omnistrategic tendrils in their work surrounding marketing, sales and IT. It's also about the people who are or strive to become leaders for big companies… who want to know what the secret sauce of the modern world *really* is.

I would also love to say that it's about the politicians seeking to promote an active industrial policy and healthy future job market, but this is the only area where I'm not entirely optimistic (I have yet to see or meet even one politician who has actually understood, or even wanted to understand, what this is all about—you'll have to see it as a challenge, I guess).

CHAPTER 2: THE FIVE DIGITAL MARKETING MEANS

What will we learn? *The five digital means: social media, display, search, site and digital CRM.*
Why is this important? *To understand their strategic significance and properties.*

Last chapter examined what has thus far fueled the explosive development of digital marketing. It has left marketers all across the globe struggling to keep up, and as a result many of them lack confidence in their digital campaigns. Their inability to realize the full potential of their digital investments can be remedied though, and the first step in that direction is to find out what tools they have at their disposal.

In this chapter we will look closer at the five digital marketing tools: social media, display, search, site and digital CRM. The chapter will clearly delineate what shape these five digital instruments take, what they have the power to do, what strategic considerations we must have in mind when using them, and their general pros and cons. Finally, we will go over some useful advice that might come in handy for the modern marketer.

DIGITAL MEANS

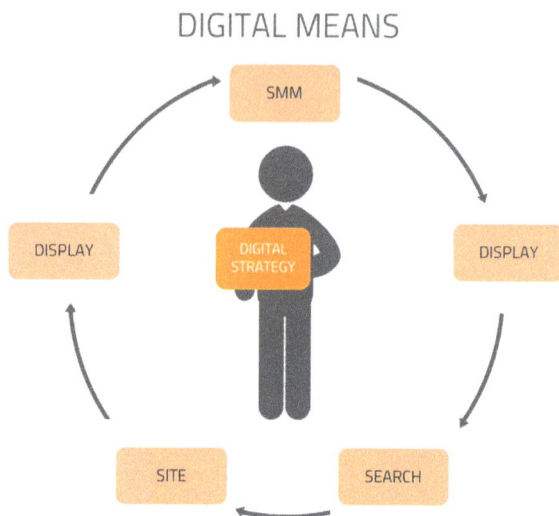

By constructing this fundamental framework, a whole lot of possibilities will suddenly emerge. We will be able to clearly see what we should and shouldn't do in our every-day marketing, and we will get a preliminary hint of what to expect in terms of return on investment.

Or in other words, what fruits a comprehensive digital marketing skillset will allow us to reap.

Social media marketing
What is social media marketing?
Social Media Marketing (SMM)—the first of our five means to be put under the microscope—is definitely one of the hotter subjects of today. Not only do alltarget audiences fre-quent social media these days, but this is also where they are the most engaged.

Channels of interest can be everything from big media platforms such as Facebook, WeChat and YouTube, to slightly narrower and fast-growing ones like Instagram, Snapchat and Pinterest, but also channels more inclined toward business, like LinkedIn and Slideshare.

In most of these channels, you use your own page as an outpost to reach out to target audiences through dialogs and posts, but you can also buy ads in order to attract potential consumers who have not yet found out about you (and if this wouldn't for some reason be possible in some channel today, then it definitely will be tomorrow).

How important is social media marketing?

SMM used to be good for some "funny money" on the side. Now it constitutes a major part of the average advertiser's digital marketing campaigns.

Which is not weird at all, of course. User-generated content now makes up two-thirds of all web pages in the world. Moreover, the fact that mobile and social media has enjoyed an exceptionally bountiful matrimony only further adds to that. The reach, frequency and intensity of social media-generated visits are in a league entirely of their own, far ahead of those of other media.

There are 2.8 billion global social media users today. About 71% of consumers who have had a good social media service experience with a brand are likely to recommend it to others. In 2015 alone, Facebook reportedly influenced over 50% of consumers' offline *and* online purchases.

This is just cherry-picking juicy statistics from a bowl overflowing with them. In just a few years, social media has truly become king of the hill. What we have is a few different platforms where almost all content is being siloed. We have gone from the tidy and methodical life as provided by business and news sites; through the anarchistic disorder of blogs and social media; to finally reuniting in enormous digital galleries to undergo gentrification. The digital media consumption, once upon a time supplied by media and business sites, with journalists and professional editorialists publishing monologs they wanted people to read and heed… is now all about social media, where people engage in actual *dialogs* with each other. The whole world of digital interaction has been turned upside down.

But even though all evidence points to the fact that social media is bursting at the seams in its rampant expansion, many companies are actually still wary about prying open their wallets where social media-fueled marketing campaigns are concerned.

Strategic considerations in social media marketing

But saying that digital interaction has been turned upside down doesn't even nearly cover it. It has been turned inside out as well. It's beyond recognition. And it is not just that business and media monologs in traditional media are being replaced with consumer dialogs in digital media—interaction has completely changed pace, place and direction.

In this regard, the strategic question of highest importance is whether to "move the mountain to Mohammed" or "move Mohammed to the mountain"—i.e. whether we should use expensive traffic-driving methods to force people to leave the safe and comfortable confines of their preferred hangouts, or relocate ourselves right to the hotspot in the midst of where all these social conversations take place.

We live in a world where the precipitous expansion of digital media has made it so very *easy to reach out*, while the tempest of media noise makes it all the more *harder to reach in*. What with the way especially the larger SMM channels have developed in recent years, the great strategic question has been *impression v/s impact.* More specifically, whether or not we should be using SMM as yet another tool for *reach media* (to make a small impression on a lot of people), or if we should use it as *engagement media* (to make a big impact on somewhat fewer people)—which the means is unique in being able to accomplish.

REACH VS ENGAGEMENT MEDIA

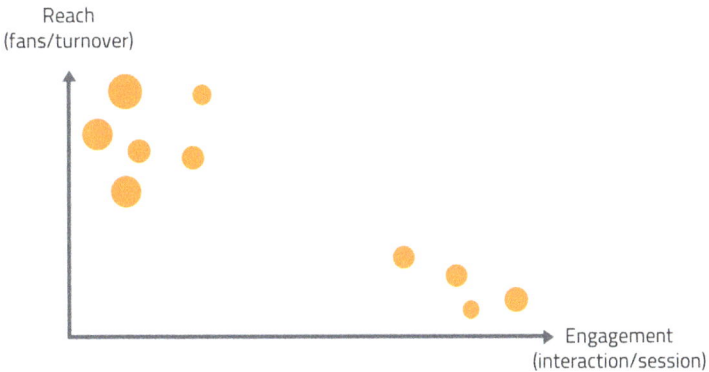

What are the pros and cons of social media marketing?

Assuming that we focus on engagement media, there are a number of highly valuable benefits of using SMM as compared to other means. You attain an unparalleled level of trust and engagement by affecting a consumer through his friends, and one might argue that this is topmost on aforementioned list of advantages. What's more, the mouth-to-mouth phenomenon of the Great Digitalization yields the additional perk of further reinforcing the message if it goes viral. Successful earned media campaigns are cheap too, of course.

And as sprinkles on top—the possibly least mentioned bonus effect—the opportunity to grow extremely wise! Taking the time to analyze both what people say and do (attitude + behavior) will generally beget such a qualitative MI (market intelligence) that it completely checkmates whatever a bunch of thousand questionnaire victims have to say about their "attitude" (i.e. what the consumers *think* they believe).

Because the thing is, with annual digital footprint in the terabyte range—that's from *one* person, by the by—SMM grants access to enormous possibilities to analyze consumer behavior. This is "big data" of such a magnitude that Zuckerberg knows that you'll break up with your significant other two months before the thought has even crossed your mindFunnily, this impact has been so strong so that while I have heard business people in Sweden ask me, "Is social media really that important?", others in South-East Asia have asked, "Is there anything else than social media that is important in digital marketing?".

Let's just pretend the first question never happened. And as regards the second: even though it is a little more along the right lines, of course the answer to it is yes. SMM does possess some unprecedented advantages, but of course there are drawbacks aplenty to go around here as well. Other means let you prognosticate the future effects of your marketing with quite some precision.[1] Social media, on the other hand, cannot boast the same kind of accuracy; you simply don't know if your posts, texts, pics, clips etc. will bring about any effect at all. One solution to that problem could be to launch several simultaneous SMM campaigns, but then you wouldn't know which one of them actually generated the effect. Likewise, you won't know *when* the effect, if any, of the campaign will occur—perhaps at the exact moment you desire… but then

---

1. If you purchase banners for $100,000 at the negotiated price of 25 CPM, you know with a fair amount of certainty that you will get around 40 million exposures with 25 million inscreens, around 1 million dwells, around 60,000 people in traffic of which at least half will be quality traffic, as well as—depending on the quality of the creatives, offers, prices, brands, landing page and conversion point—about 500–3000 conversions.

again, it might come weeks after your campaign is over, or even when the product has been removed from stock.

What's more, SMM is seldom the solution to all problems; if the rest of the earned media isn't cooperating efficiently enough, the whole SMM campaign will collapse.[2] And even though earned media is technically "free of charge", the greatest effect is achieved when bought media is used as the catalyst to bought media—so not treated well it's not really that free after all.

Finally, there is that most important, most obvious and usually least accepted fact to contend with—SMM is a high-maintenance means. If you want to use social media, you have to be social, or there is no point being there. Organizationally speaking, you are looking at quite an exhaustive effort whether you outsource it or do it inhouse (though the latter is to prefer). In addition to that, responsibility and HR is not everything either; for SMM to work you need follow-ups, system support and structured, thorough operations.

Golden insight #1: If you are on social media, you have to be social. Otherwise there is no point being there.

Display advertising
What is display advertising?
Even though SMM isn't exactly a spring chicken anymore, it is still a hot discussion and budget topic for marketers. Display, on the other hand, has practically been around since the beginning of time, or possibly longer. The first "banner" popped up about a year after the conception of the World Wide Web in 1994, effectively making display the oldest

2. The consumer stumbles on something interesting on a fanpage or Instapic, googles it and must find *your* company amid all the others— otherwise you would do a competitor a favor. The consumer then reaches a site that has to be attractive enough for him not to immediately leave.

offsite digital traffic-driving tool. Thanks to this early pioneering ad, most people still think of banners when they hear digital marketing.

PROS AND CONS OF SMM

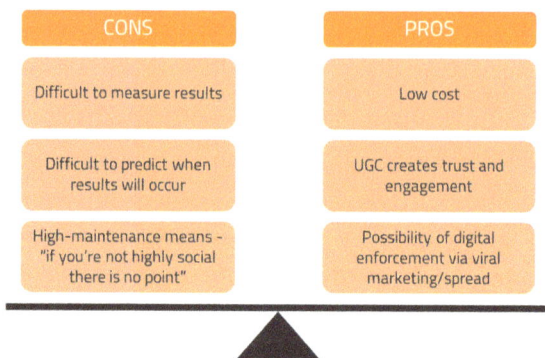

CONS	PROS
Difficult to measure results	Low cost
Difficult to predict when results will occur	UGC creates trust and engagement
High-maintenance means - "if you're not highly social there is no point"	Possibility of digital enforcement via viral marketing/spread

The essence of display marketing is "banners" used to exhibit digital information and interaction in close proximity to editorial content on various "media" sites. These sites more or less incorporate all places not social media, search engine or individual company pages, such as traditional media sites, price comparison sites, link sites, e-commerce sites etc. The message is exposed in large panorama formats and natives, to small "banners" and everything in between, as well as creatives in the form of rich media, video banners, mobile ads, static "print ads", etc.

How important is display advertising?

Banners offer great potential for achieving vast reach, and with a steeply growing internet penetration that is showing no sign of stopping, it is still at big tool for marketers—a trend that has held true ever since the advent of digital marketing. In fact, it has constituted such a large focus for marketers that banners have come to embody the very essence of what digital marketing is. Ever since the beginning of the second millennium, display has been one of the two largest constituents of digital marketing.

Strategic considerations in display marketing

Today though, a much smaller part of the population is de facto reachable via banners. To blame are things like banner blindness, which are decreasing the number of actual observations, and adblockers, which are eliminating exposure entirely and thus drastically decreasing the number of impressions as a whole. By the end of the last year, there were a total of 615 million devices blocking ads worldwide. One would think the number of investments in banners might dwindle because of this. This, however, is not the case. Instead, the big difference is the transition from old banners to video banners and especially mobile advertisements.

The strategic question which arises is whether or not to drive traffic. First of all, if you "have to" drive traffic in order to reach other goals such as engagement and conversion, then you should. But if it is possible to reserve traffic-driving actions for the instances when there are certain tangible conversions you want the consumer to do (become a lead, buy something, or otherwise activate in some way), then that is preferable.

In the first case, there is today decent support for strong awareness via rich media and video advertisement in the banner itself (doesn't require any click-through). In the second, demand side platform (DSP) and affiliate networks provide new solutions to maximize return on investment (ROI) on click, through behavioral control and retargeting. There are also currencies where you pay either via real time bidding (RTB) or for the result (CPA/CPL/CPO) instead of the "possibility" of it.

Other equally important considerations in the realm of

display marketing concern things like the means' enormous possibilities. Within *media* how seldom true AI-optimization to achieve maximum balance of customer value and business advantage is performed. Within *creative*how seldom it is designed to provide interaction in the actual banner itself, and thus eliminate the need for a consumer to migrate to another platform or website—all in true digital spirit.

What are the pros and cons of display advertising?

Despite its esteemed age, display as a digital marketing tool still has its uses. For one, it is a type of creative that many intuitively understand—it is basically digital versions of traditional ads and TVCs. It is also a smorgasbord for the creatively inclined, filled with morsels like graphic images, animation, copy, questionnaires and interactive design that are all well-equipped to stimulate more senses than just the visual.

That display can be bought in performance-based currencies like cost per action (CPA) from affiliate networks and programmatic is yet another perk, but then it is still vital to continually measure and compare against the ROI of all other traffic-driving alternatives. When working with display, it is also possible to determine, and thus "know", the extent of the outcome.Through retargeting, you can concentrate the ads on only the people who have, for instance, already visited your site. That way, ushering them yet another step in the consumer journey is easier and more likely to succeed.

But just like with SMM, there is a darker flipside to display as well. The number of people using traditional digital media is constantly decreasing, and what few do are prone to such information overload that actually reaching through to consumers is becoming harder and harder. Between adblockers, banner blindness and the fact that the average consumer in a mature market is exposed to 1700–2000 banners every month, it's not exactly hard to see why seizing the attention of consumers is difficult.

To make matters worse, the few people who even see the banners in the first place are nowadays less disposed to "transport" themselves to another digital place—something which is clearly illustrated by CTR having dropped from 2% in 2000 to 0.04% in 2017. Moreover, these clicks originate from a very small part of the population, with 85% of all clicks coming from 8% of all exposed people.

But the thing is, all of this would essentially be resolved if we—the advertisers—actually utilized the many benefits of CPA currencies. Despite that, many agencies stubbornly purchase the "possibility" of result (CPM) instead of the actual result itself (CPA) in their sales campaigns. Consequently, the entire register of previously mentioned negative trends sets in (like lower visit frequency on traditional digital media, increased banner blindness, increased usage of adblockers, less motivation to transfer, etc.). No wonder advertisers' ROIs shrink.

If this mean is to survive, the industry needs to engage in some serious pruning.

PROS AND CONS OF DISPLAY

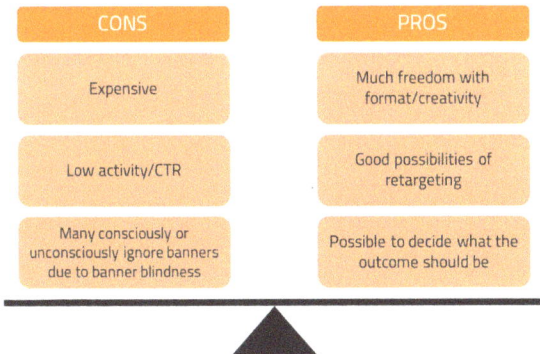

CONS	PROS
Expensive	Much freedom with format/creativity
Low activity/CTR	Good possibilities of retargeting
Many consciously or unconsciously ignore banners due to banner blindness	Possible to decide what the outcome should be

Search engine marketing
What is search engine marketing?

If SMM is the hot talk of the town, and display the venerable old-timer, then search lies somewhere in between. And while SMM is a half-decent traffic-driver, and correctly executed display advertising is even better still, search is the actual king in this regard. If that's what you're looking for, of course—but more on that later.

Search engine marketing—i.e. maximizing the probability that consumers searching for products and services find *your* company and not your competitors—is simply a hyper-potent marketing tool. Google rules this world with over 85% of all global search traffic, with "competitors" like Bing (5%) and Yahoo (4%) trying their best to keep up, while Baidu rules the Chinese market.

Search engine marketing is done in two different ways: via organic index (SEO = Search Engine Optimization) or bought search ads (SEM = Search Engine Marketing).

In the former of the two—the organic index—the search engines rank the hits based on algorithms that calculate what pages have the highest relevance for the words or phrases consumers search for. As a means to this end, Google and other search engines send out so-called "spiders" that virtually act as fake people. The spiders assess how well-suited a particular website is for a potential consumer looking for a specific search word or phrase, and then ranks it according to the estimated relevance.

Working with SEO is all about creating good content correlation. Your "promise" to the spiders (via metatags, descriptions, domains, site title, etc.), and your "delivery" in the form of content (text, headings, images, etc.) must be in as much harmony as possible. In the past, the number of links to each respective page was also a variable of importance, but nowadays its significance has deflated considerably—partly because of the fact that mobile is responsible for more than 60% of all searches, and partly because people abused the system by buying links.

Bought ads (SEM) is a different story though. The point here is to create small and very simple ads (50–60 characters) that include a heading and a call-2-action (C2A). The difference being that if you have enough money, you will always rank well in the search engine result page (SERP). The question is whether it is worth it in terms of ROI. Just like with display.

Again, it is return vs investment—how much you think a visitor who has searched for a particular word/phrase is worth to you and your company vs. what you think a reasonable investment in a visit from that person isThis ROI calculation results in a number (CPC = Cost Per Click) and functions as your bid in RTB auctions, where you contest other auctioneers (your competitors) for the traffic of the relevant consumers. In other words, we have a fully transparent price mechanism showing what competitors think various types of visitors are worth, and this is what you must weigh against what *you* think they are worth.

How important is search engine marketing?

If a more action-oriented type of marketing appeals to you, the significance of search is hard to match. Every year, Google processes over 2000 billion searches from all across the globe. More importantly though, a large part of all these searches are in one way or another business related. People who search are usually well on their way along their customer journeys. The effectiveness of SEO is even such that it generates 14.6% conversion as opposed to DM and print (1.7%). Some 82% consider search engines important tools when purchasing things online, while eight out of ten use the web for ROPO (Research Online Purchase Offline)—i.e. searching for a specific item in a search engine, getting a feel for the product and then purchasing it in a physical store. Consequently, search has become an incredibly influential instrument not only for online sales, but also—and perhaps even more so—for offline sales.

As a kind of mirror version, there is also Showrooming, which is conducting research in a physical store before purchasing the product online. According to a local study, every other consumer says that they have at least once during the last six months examined an item in a physical store and then procured it on the internet. In another study spanning 188 countries, online (67%) was ranked almost as high as offline (72%) for shopping. And how does the process start? With search.

This has made search popular among marketers, and with good reason too. Of the two general search techniques, the organic index is indubitably the most important one, since eight out of ten consumers click on those search hits. In other words, not only is SEO "free", but it also has the highest reach and credibility—and thus, a greater power of influence.

Despite that, SEO, as opposed to SEM, has yet to really reach its full potential with marketers. In large, this is likely because of the hands-down fantastic salesmanship of our friends at Google, in combination with their customarily very bountiful relations with our other friends the media agencies.

Strategic considerations in search engine marketing

Strategically, one of the most important things is allocating at least as much focus to SEO as SEM, since it's free, yields a greater reach and generates significantly higher credibility. However, on one hand throwing money at expensive SEO consultants every once in a while is not nearly as productive a route to take as making sure the people responsible for site content start including the SEO routine in their everyday work.

When time comes to use SEM on the other hand, the

assessment must be grounded in completely different criteria (CPA, CPL, CPO, CPQ[3]) than the currency used to trade in (CPC). For way too long now, the trend has instead been to "CPC-minimize", a mode of procedure that tends to result in traffic that, while being cheap, is of low quality. Meanwhile, those who try to "CPA-minimize" usually get the results they are actually interested in, as cheaply as is possible.[4]

What are the pros and cons of search engine marketing?

The main advantages of search engine marketing is that it is both highly effective and has the potential for enormous traffic. Weaving SEO into the site tends to elevate traffic considerably.

What's more, the consumers you attract have often come a long way in their customer journeys and are practically just waiting to be converted. Another benefit is that by using the "right" search word, there is a decent possibility of catching people who have never before searched for your specific brand.

Finally, SEO is free and SEM is easily analyzed and budgeted.

But of course—as we have previously discovered—there are drawbacks with search engine marketing too. First of all, the technical aspect of SEO is not all. Even hiring a link farm to improve a page's search engine ranking is not enough. Infusing your site's structure with relevant SEO takes hard work and resources in terms of HR, and it has to be done consistently in order for it to be effective.

Everything else is just temporary solutions, since SEO requires old pages to be continuously kept up to date, implementation on new ones, and a constant stream of relevant content to make sure there is a good correlation to the most important keywords. Like SMM, SEO can't "guarantee" traffic, which means it can never

---

3. Cost per quality.

4. Within CPO/CPA-minimization we instead approach another problem concerned with LTV (lifetime value), but more regarding that later on.

be a "sure thing" in a budget. And while SEO is practically free, SEM has the tendency to grow quite expensive.

By CPC-minimizing instead of focusing on CPA, you also run the risk of getting kind of distorted results. There is the peril of later suboptimization here. The more you focus on low costs for "investment" in quantitative terms, the more you compromise the "return" in qualitative terms.

PROS AND CONS OF SEM

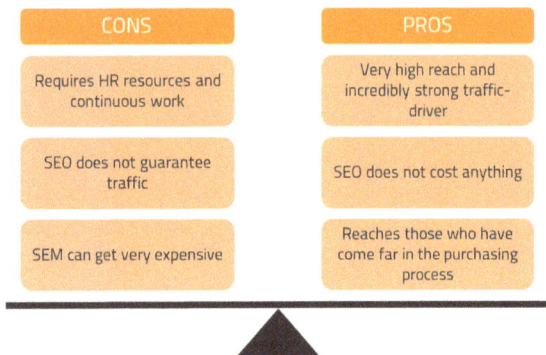

CONS	PROS
Requires HR resources and continuous work	Very high reach and incredibly strong traffic-driver
SEO does not guarantee traffic	SEO does not cost anything
SEM can get very expensive	Reaches those who have come far in the purchasing process

Site strategy
What is a site strategy?
Having concluded the chapters on the three traffic-driving activities SMM, display and search, we have now arrived at the very core of traditional digital marketing—the company's website. In fact, site is so ancient that when it originally came about, it was usually nothing more than brochures directly uploaded to the web… and in some cases only fully text-based pages with information about the company.

Since then, site has undergone an extreme makeover, both in terms of design and significance. Even so, its function is yet more or less the same—it is a place to where you drive traffic, both via online and offline media, and present "content" designed to boost either a company's brand or business.

And so, our fourth digital marketing means is our old partner-in-crime site, whose role in the big scheme of things is *traffic management*. It functions as a sort of landing page for the three previously described *traffic-driving* means. The challenge here is to make sure that both the relevance of the site's content and the appeal of its design are so high that people choose to stay long enough to activate themselves—and this irrespective of where the traffic originates from, be it social media, display, search or as direct traffic. What we want to do here is to bring the customer to a logical terminus (LT) as quickly as possible, by guiding him through a kind of cookie crumb trail absent any cul-de-sacs (CDS), and with as few preparatory transit routes (TR) as possible.

The old way of achieving this is through a so-called vertical traffic strategy (VTS) via a front page. The somewhat more modern and productive way is to lead the consumer to a LT via a horizontal traffic strategy (HTS). The latter method requires the site to be blueprinted in a way so that virtually every page can be construed as a front page.

It doesn't matter if your site is a simple webpage or a complex product catalog, an extensive e/m-commerce or just a digital landing page; the challenge lies in getting consumers to stay on the site when they visit (= minimizing bounce), and then provide search paths sufficiently straightforward and attractive for the consumers to find what they are looking for (= maximizing activity). This must be supplemented with carefully thought-out conversion points (= optimizing conversion) that help consumers take the next step in their BAC process (bounce → activity → conversion).

MODEL FOR SITE STRATEGY

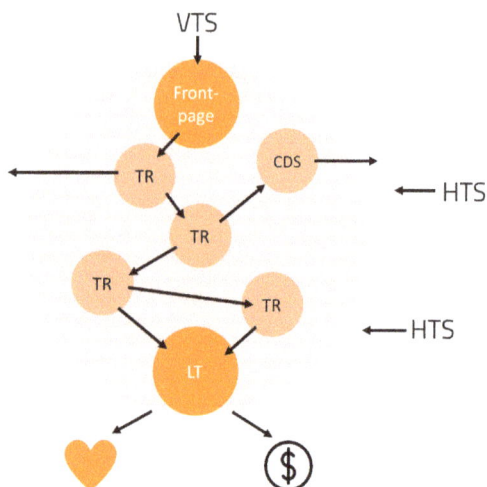

Golden insight #2: Optimize the site, with focus on minimizing bounce, maximizing activity and optimizing conversion (BAC): bounce → activity → conversion.

How important is a site strategy?

The importance of the site's role is still to this day discussed. All data points to the fact that consumers are getting more and more disinclined to transport themselves from their platforms of choice (social media, news sites, etc.) and that it is becoming increasingly difficult to shepherd consumers to companies' own, often highly ethnocentric sites. It has been a long time since the digital strategy went from a "me-perspective" to a weigendian "we-perspective".

The most blatant piece of evidence for this is the drastically decreased click frequency on banners, which has plummeted from the 2% we saw at the end of the last millennium, to the

0.04% we have today—which equates to a massive 50 times decline. Another sign is the high levels of bounce rate coming from traffic generated by social media.

That being said, the site plays a major role for most companies, and is often considered the heart of the digital ecosystem. With things like the mobile explosion, which has cranked up mobile internet usage to the point where it has actually surpassed desktop usage; countries like Iceland whose mobile internet penetration is a weird 100%; and the fact that e-commerce (and accordingly, also m-commerce) is as of 2017 a multi-trillion ($) business, it is small wonder that site is considered to be as important as it is.

But unlike SEO, the importance of site is today common knowledge amid companies. Content is often being handled internally by inhouse teams, although form and function is still being mostly outsourced. The typical budget for content marketing is growing as well, as marketers gain more and more insight in how good content and site campaigns generate substantial ROI:al effects.

Strategic considerations for site

The first two questions are *a)* do I really have to drive traffic? and *b)* what role does SMM play for site? Does the former channel corral suspects and turn them into prospects, while the latter converts prospects to actual customers? Or is SMM primarily for softer things such as customer care and cuddling with the consumers' hearts, while site is for more need-2-know things chiefly intended for the brain—more specifically, the classical digital chain of *information* (product specifications, guarantees, etc.), *interaction* (customer service) and *transaction* (e-commerce/store locator)?

Dealing with the issue of too much dependence on external agencies, not only when it comes to its development but also for the daily administration and optimization, is yet another challenge, though of more tactical nature. Lately, as content management systems (CMSs) are becoming more advanced and dynamic while retaining high user-friendliness, this issue is at least in the process of being resolved. Likewise, the expansion of easy-to-use AB/MV-testing systems measuring the strength and relevance of *form* (navigation, layout, functionalities, funnels, etc.) and various types of *content* (subjects, text lengths, headers, pictures and clips) has also aided on that note.

For that reason, it is getting much easier for companies to allocate a lot of the site work to inhouse teams, as these people will nowadays be able to produce highly relevant, dynamic and functional sites, yielding much larger effect to a notably smaller price. But what is really interesting to note is that the synergetic development on the system side of things is mirrored by an equal kind of synergy going on over on the HR side. The combination between user-friendly CMS's for content and AB/MV-systems for optimization has, in a sheer organizational sense, led to a profitable symbiosis between roles such as content managers for content and web analysts for optimization. The most developed frontrunner companies even have the combination role "contemizers"—experts at both content production and the optimization of it.

DEVELOPMENT PROCESS NOW AND THEN

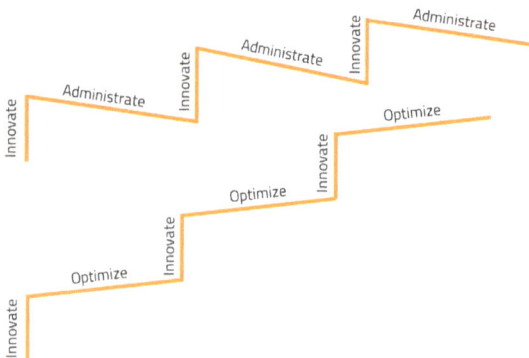

All innumerable audits I have performed over the years have made one thing abundantly clear: this is something *no one* should miss out on. This is highlighted all the more in external studies showing that only 28% of marketers are satisfied with their conversion—yet even so, only 50% perform an analysis of the consumer journey (whereas those who do increase their sales with an average of 79%).

What are the pros and cons of site strategy?

That site is a means replete with advantages probably doesn't come as a surprise. Site strategy is instrumental to attracting new prospects, but also activating existing customers. The means is an imperative component of the value chain, and often plays a critical role as the heart of the digital ecosystem.

By using a dynamic CMS, you won't be as dependent on external agencies or IT distributors, and can do a major portion, if not all of the work yourself, which in turn entails a considerably decreased cost and the possibility to have a much more dynamic site. Furthermore, basing analyses and testing on data-driven insights, you will also be able to evaluate and optimize the site yourself, which means that actively controlling the outcome becomes easier.By using responsive design, the site will also be adapted to various screen resolutions, platforms and orientations, resulting in a highly professional customer experience.

At the same time, the site has its share of drawbacks. As we went over earlier, driving traffic to a site is becoming increasingly difficult, given the fact that consumers are becoming less prone to moving from their "chosen" platforms—platforms that are effectively filtering all content for its consumers. For that reason alone, it might be more effective to "move" all conversations and commerce to the place where the consumers actually are.

And even though easy-to-use CMSs and AB/MV-systems have made inhouse management of content and optimization ("contemization") much more convenient, development, launching and maintenance of the site still requires a lot of resources, both in terms of time and money for licenses and possible retainers for external agencies. The optimization itself also demands a certain level of expertise, as well as a dynamic CMS in order to keep the site as continuously updated as is necessary to justify its place in the digital ecosystem.

Finally, if working with content marketing means adapting content for different devices, you are looking at a much tougher and more resource-intensive job. In the process create → edit → publish, the workload for the last two grows substantially when adapting content for various devices, and when personalizing the content as well, the first one also swells dramatically.

PROS AND CONS OF SITE STRATEGY

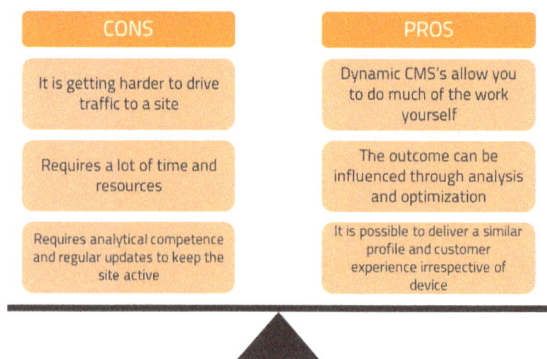

CONS	PROS
It is getting harder to drive traffic to a site	Dynamic CMS's allow you to do much of the work yourself
Requires a lot of time and resources	The outcome can be influenced through analysis and optimization
Requires analytical competence and regular updates to keep the site active	It is possible to deliver a similar profile and customer experience irrespective of device

Digital CRM
What is a digital CRM?
Our fifth tool is digital CRM, whose champion is email marketing (EMM). Like several of our previous means, it is a traffic-driving tool, although the prime difference here is that we won't, unlike social media, display and search, post an ad/image and then reactively "wait around" for some anonymous person to click it. Quite on the contrary, we proactively send content to specific individuals who have actually asked us to do it—in other words, we are doing acceptable "house calls" at the virtual residences of our customers. This usually happens through newsletters, triggers, alerts, push notifications, etc.—essentially any way we can send information to the consumers who have requested it. This information can be anything from long newsletters to simple two-three line alerts, pics and clips, polls, or anything else interactive.

How important is digital CRM?
Even though there are currently several other very interesting channels on the rise, not the least of which is mobile, email marketing still takes all the others to school. It doesn't matter how "cool" apps and chats are, it is hard to turn a blind eye to the fact that emailing is still the world's most used digital medium (even trumping APD[5] on that note).

Today, over 270 billion emails are being sent. Just today. In Sweden, 96% of the population read emails and 74% do it on a daily basis. And the remaining 4% that don't? Well, it's hard to imagine them as being anything but very young or old people.

Unlike the usual talk conveyed on trendy courses and lectures, the growth of EMM is still going strong. Unnerving rumors might claim that teenagers are not using email

5. *Analogue Printing Device*, digital nerd jargon.

anymore, but these rumors don't take into account that young people have yet to start working. As private users they haven't started the habit of reading emails—here we can instead see that chat dominates most of the private sector. That being said, email is still undoubtedly the most well-used digital means of communication within the professional sector.

Still the value of EMM lies not so much in its reach, as in its massive ROI-potential —in an American study it was shown that $1 invested generates a return of $40, and 67% of all marketers there consider EMM to be the strongest of all channels.

Despite the very clear evidence of prowess that digital CRM exhibits—and particularly its subgenre EMM—the means is not exactly getting the attention it deserves. Last year, I personally hosted 25 lectures with engaging topics such as SMM, trendspotting, mobile advertisement and similar hot themes… but not once was I asked to talk about EMM—it's just not sexy enough. People simply see it as an old-school gadget that has been around since forever, and there is no glory in a tool that is responsible for generating so much "spam" for so many people over the years.

But—and this is an important but—there is a reason why it actually still *is* around.

Therefore, in a purely emotional sense, EMM isn't very highly prioritized by marketers. But basing one's business on emotions is a precarious road to tread. Rationally speaking, the few marketers who actually take the means seriously are laughing all the way to the bank.

Despite the clearly demonstrable value of digital CRM and/or EMM, it still doesn't constitute a major portion of companies' budget. For allt the hundreds ofcompanies I have been working with over the recent years—and these are considered rather foresighted companies too—the budget allocation reserved for CRM and EMM has averaged around a pesky single%.

This can of course be partially explained by the means being so very cheap, but the primary reason is likely that there is no intimate third party actively advocating for or trying to sell it, like for banners, FB ads or adwords, where most marketers these days are completely bombarded by their agencies trying to get in on the action.

My personal experience with hundreds of marketers has shown that this is more about being able to provide business cases than anything else. It is all about proving the effects of proposed projects in structured scenario analyses, and then develop strategies that don't rely on spam—spam that only results in badwill anyway—but actual digital CRM with applied as 1-2-1-marketing—which resluts in goodwill instead. Even though CRM isn't a particularly expensive means, it might be worth investing that extra dollar in order to convert bad EMM to fantastic EMM.

Strategic considerations for digital CRM

CRM is gaining ground; it is an important tool today, but tomorrow it will be even more crucial. It is a well-known truth today that we are exposed to thousands of ads every day (digital marketing experts in the US estimate that most Americans are exposed to around 4000 to 10,000 advertisements every day). As the media noise is expanding out of control, the importance of digital CRM will completely take over.

When consumers are more or less drowning in information, it will become harder to reel them in. Today, you will already manifold your ROI by focusing on existing customers instead of trying to seduce new ones. Tomorrow? Again, this is something that will only keep increasing in importance.

Add to this the fact that social media is practically already holding the reins of media consumption—a trend not very likely to change—and that one of its chief functions for us as marketers is that we gain further value from customers through both their "virility" (consumption value) and "virality" (social value). The conclusion to be drawn from all of this is that digital CRM, in its most modern state—"social CRM"—will evolve to comprise the very heart and soul of every company aiming for digital success.

FROM "ONE SIZE FITS ALL" TO 1-2-1

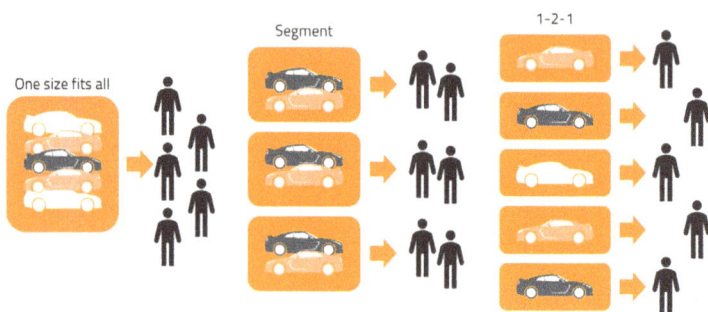

And if we also incorporate the enormous possibilities of advanced big data systems for the analysis of digital and analog touchpoints (=digalog touchpoints) to match suitable content to each individual—then we have something as incredible as a self-playing piano with omnichannel-flavor and total personalization 1-2-1 via marketing automation...

... bringing us *far* away from the old-school spam-based emails inciting nothing but badwill, and instead allowing us to supply consumers with glamorous alerts generating goodwill.

What are the pros and cons of digital CRM?

Utilizing digital CRM—and especially EMM—is a very cheap and effective way of reaching out to the large number of "warm" customers who have already shown interest. There are simply many advantages here.

The level of targeting and personalized interaction that is possible with CRM allows for communication tailored for each target audience, and sometimes even for each individual—something that no other means has previously been able to do.

ROI can be further increased by using CRM systems that allow for analysis and optimization. The means also has the power to nail down the "window shoppers" who haven't come long enough in their customer journeys to be ready for purchase. Sending a message, especially if it is personalized, might also motivate both loyalty in the target audience/individual as well as a desire to return.

But there are of course also disadvantages. Apart from leads generation, digital CRM/EMM is not exactly optimal for managing new customers, since its application often requires explicit approval from the consumers for the marketer to be able to send anything to them in the first place. What's more, without the right level of personalization there is a risk that the EMM might be seen as spam, which obviously hurts the brand by creating badwill instead of goodwill.

Lastly, there is usually rather limited elbow room for creativity.

PROS AND CONS OF DIGITAL CRM

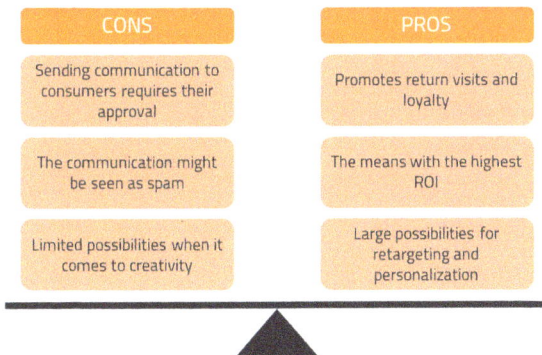

CONS	PROS
Sending communication to consumers requires their approval	Promotes return visits and loyalty
The communication might be seen as spam	The means with the highest ROI
Limited possibilities when it comes to creativity	Large possibilities for retargeting and personalization

Summary

We have seen how the digital marketing techniques have been divided in five parts—five essential components of marketing, five digital means. The first component, *social media marketing* (SMM), is one of the hottest marketing topics of today and can be used as reach media for both bought and earned traffic, as well as engagement media. The advantages are many and great, and the means is singular in its ability to spur engagement and a strong sense of credibility in consumers. On the other hand, we have some pretty serious drawbacks like uncertain prognostication.

The second component is *display* (also sometimes referred to as "banners"). Display is essentially digital advertising in the form of large panorama banners and small strips, rich media and video banners, mobile advertisement and simple "print ads" on the web. One of the greatest perks of display, except reach and penetration, is its measurability and possibilities for digital interaction. On the other side of the scale are things like banner blindness and decreased interactivity.

The third tool is the hyper-potent effects generated by *search engine marketing* in terms of both earned traffic (SEO) and bought traffic (SEM). These are purely traffic-driving measures with strong interaction with site. There are many advantages of successful search engine marketing—for instance, the ability to reach consumers who have already come far in their customer journeys and are all but ready to seal the deal. Some of the drawbacks are that earned traffic is hard to successfully acquire, while bought traffic can punch large holes in the budget.

The fourth digital marketing tool is *site*, which could be everything from a simple webpage to a complex e-/m-commerce, a campaign site or any other kind of digital landing page. Site is usually considered to be the heart of the digital ecosystem. No chain is stronger than its weakest link though, and therefore site is most often a must-have. But even though there are many possibilities with site, it is getting harder to drive traffic to an ego-site where the company itself is in focus, especially since consumers are more likely to stay on the platforms they like, and generally tend to refrain from transporting themselves elsewhere.

And finally, our fifth means is *digital CRM*—traditionally made up of EMM. The means is amid the best tools for sharpshooting and personalization through custom-tailored interaction sent straight into individual customers' email inboxes/mobiles/apps. One of the disadvantages of CRM is the fact that we need the customer's express approval to be allowed to do the kinds of "house calls" required for CRM to truly work. It is also quite demanding resource-wise, due to constant content personalization—something which is crucial for the interaction not to be seen as spam.

To sum things up, we have five extremely strong digital tools that are all great at different things, in different contexts, for differently sized companies and for different goals. The big question is: which is most important for you and your situation? The name of the solution is *digital strategy*, which also happens to be the topic for the next chapter.

CHAPTER 3: THE PATH TO SUCCESS IS PAVED WITH DIGITAL STRATEGY

What will we learn? *How to develop a digital strategy by using a tried-and-true 7-step process.*
Why is this important? *To ensure the highest possibility of success, using the least amount of resources, in the minimal amount of time.*

As we have seen, each of the five digital marketing tools have their own advantageous functions, and are all well worth investing both resources and competence in. However, it doesn't matter how fast you run if you don't know which way you're going (in reality, putting all your energy into running as fast as possible will more likely than not only result in you arriving quicker at the wrong destination). In order to decide what the best direction is, the development of a digital strategy is absolutely vital.

In the coming chapter, this is precisely what we will learn—how to build a sound digital strategy. We will familiarize ourselves with a 7-step process specifically designed for the development of a digital strategy. It includes how to identify goals and means that work best for specific situations and setups; how to perform a matching of means; how to adapt the strategy to an organization or a budget; how to identify synergies and redundancies with other strategies; and finally how to develop a thorough activity plan for the practical implementation (this entire process can also be learned from the wolds' most installed independent app within the subject, "Digital Marketing Pro" (DMP), downloadable as IOS or Android from App Store/Google Play or at www.aiar.com).

7-STEP PROCESS FOR DIGITAL STRATEGY DEVELPOMENT

Strategic platform ➡ Goals analysis ➡ Means analysis ➡ Digital matching ➡ Moment of truth ➡ Moment of strategy ➡ Digital roadmap

All in order to create optimal conditions for developing a digital strategy that has the greatest possibility of success, using the least amount of resources in the minimal amount of time.

Step 1: Strategic platform
The motive behind the first step

The platform underlying the entire digital strategy requires us to first take stock of the strategic prerequisites behind the digital campaigns. The person who is used to looking forward rather than backward might wonder why, but the answer is simple—and very important: one of the worst fates that can befall a digital strategy is that it becomes a silo, utterly isolated from other strategies and company processes. The second worst result of the strategic work is that too much time and resources are wasted on analysis—there is actually very little need to reinvent the wheel.[6]

Externally there are commonly prior analyses of the market,

---

6. Practically the only thing that can compete as a worst-case scenario here is that external parties with vested interests in the nature of the strategy get too much leeway, or if organizational politics get out of hands—but more on that soon.

target audiences, distributors, competitors and other influential parties that can be consulted. *Internally*, interviewing strategically important persons and examining various types of business strategies, GAP analyses, organizational analyses and similar things are common—and profitable—practice.

Based on this material, we can perform an initial outlining of the foundation on which the digital strategy will be erected, including purpose, organization, budget and other strategies, as well as internal and external analyses relevant to the strategy development. In essence, we are taking stock of what we have today, and what research will have to generated to make the strategy robust.

The expected result here is a thorough analytical and strategic platform which will help guide us through decisions regarding what the strategic development will come to require.

Companies who know their existing strategies well usually get started much quicker, while more action-oriented growth companies that are less strategically inclined take a little longer. Irrespective, the end result is an instructive inventory of both what we have *today* and what we will have to acquire to realize our goals *tomorrow*.

Strategic platform 1

Analysis of the strategic platform that will constitute the foundation of the entire digital strategy.

1. Take stock of what you have, and create an initial outline of the background behind the digital strategy, including its purpose, the organization, other strategies, as well as internal and external analyses relevant to the development of the digital strategy.

2. Take stock of what you have and what additional research is needed in order to make the strategy robust.

Step 2: Goals analysis
The motive behind the second step

Thus far our strategic platform encompasses only the background of our company and the purpose of our digital strategy in the making. The first "real" step in the strategic development is about something completely different though, and is possibly the most crucial part of the digital strategy development.

In the previous chapter, we examined the five digital marketing tools to quite some extent, including what impact they have on our marketing campaigns—and by extension, our business. We also discussed some strategic considerations to keep in mind when using them and a few of their general pros and cons.

But the thing is, it doesn't really matter how "efficient" you are with each means (= how fast you're running). It is much more important to be aware of what means are the most contributory to your specific company's prioritized goals (= which direction to run). The most important step in the journey to a fully functional digital strategy is therefore to specify both the intended target audience and the digital goals most suitable for them.

Specifying goals and target audience is obviously not exclusive to digital marketing. One might believe that this process can be done in the same way as it is in the analog realm, but there are actually a number of important variables to bear in mind when dealing with *online* as opposed to *offline*.

The first and possibility greatest advantage of digital marketing is that it enables a phenomenal level of surgical warfare. By working online, we can identify where the greatest media consumption (Channel) of each respective segment (Customer) is, and in what context consumers tend to be the most susceptible (Context) for various types of messages (Communication).

DIGITAL STRATEGY DEVELOPMENT

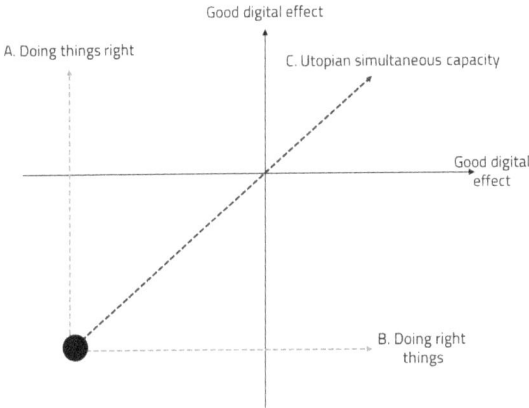

Good digital effect

A. Doing things right

C. Utopian simultaneous capacity

Good digital effect

B. Doing right things

Digital marketing also gives us the opportunity to very narrowly pinpoint where exactly in the branding/purchasing process the consumer currently is. And if we can do such a thing, then obviously we should—if the alternative is wildly firing shotgun blasts in all directions in desperate attempts to hit everything or anything, we might just as well throw our money away.

Another benefit of the digital tools is that we can achieve certain types of goals much easier than offline. Some of the digital marketing means are almost as good at creating awareness as offline means. However, there are very few traditional means that can match the digital ones at engaging consumers, driving traffic or instigating some desired action. There is no contest—digital marketing is in a league of its own. It is superior at realizing narrow and specific goals, but it can also serve a complementary role in a seamless omnichannel strategy by synchronizing with other market activities.

How do we do this?

As regards the specification of the *digital target audience*, you will find that there are excellent possibilities for targeting. Remember, those who try to reach everyone usually end up reaching no one.

> **Golden insight #3:** Those who try to reach everyone usually end up reaching no one.

On one side of the board, we see the marketing director who is still trapped in traditional media; who is blindly firing his shotgun in hope of hitting anything at all; and who might have, at the very most, started dabbling with segmentation. On the other side are those who use modern technology and techniques to wind their personalization all the way up to the 1-2-1 level. And the narrower we aim (= lower quantity), the more important it is that we are absolutely certain we are shooting at the right target (= higher quality). Preferably, this strategic analysis should be performed via a 3-stageanalysis, where the digital target audience is identified based on three different dimensions:

1. *Consumer needs:* what types of consumers or companies are likely to want our services and products, what characterizes these people, and what are their consumption behaviors?

2. *Purchasing power:* who is most likely to purchase a product (in the case of e.g. slow-moving durable goods), or—even better—several of them (in the case of e.g. FMCG)?

3. *Social status:* who has the largest social network and persuasion power? Do they have potential to influence others with e.g. reviews?

TARGET AUDIENCE ANALYSIS

Segment	Share of market	Purchasing power	Social status	Digital focus
Target audience A	40%	1	1	15%
Target audience B	20%	3	3	20%
Target audience C	10%	2	5	20%
Target audience D	10%	5	1	25%

The first two dimensions are not so very different from analog marketing, except for the fact that they are extremely easy to identify, execute and optimize. However, it is the third dimension that really makes the difference; study upon study shows how viral marketing is unequivocally supreme compared to other types.

The average number of friends on Facebook is well above 300. The sheer possibilities for virality when it comes to a user with 1000 or more are needless to say many. You could say that the value of attracting people who are active on social media is proportional to their number of online followers or friends. Simply put, the traditional two-dimensional analysis is obsolete on its own, since the modern, successful digital strategy adheres to yet another dimension, where the target audience is not only actively contributing to its own consumption, but also that of others.

When it comes to the *digital goals*, the allocation of resources and focus between "branding" and "business" quite effectively mirrors that of the offline process. On the one hand, we have brand-driving activities intended to influence the consumer's heart and mind—seduce them in other words. On the other hand, we have business-driving activities designed to generate sales—basically get customers to open their wallets and purchase a specific service or product. In the former case we seek to affect thoughts, and in the latter to incite concrete action—i.e. attitude vs behavior.

If I ask an esteemed marketing director to rate the importance of branding on a scale from 1 to 5, he or she will say 5, or at the very least 4—there is no way a company could sell a product to a customer who doesn't trust a company, or isn't even aware of its existence in the first place. If I ask the very same marketing director to rate the importance of business, the answer will be 4 or 5 here as well—after all, business is paying the salaries.

Obviously, in terms of resource allocation, this kind of distribution is not compatible. Experience in this field has revealed a certain methodology to be far superior in this regard, and this is it:

You will start by allocating 100% between the meta-goals *branding* and *business*. Then you divide both branding and business into subgoals. , in digital strategy the first subgoal in branding is usually *awareness*, which is the very first step in brand recognition and is the prerequisite for the other subgoals—i.e. awareness of the existence of a brand and its products/services.

AWARENESS

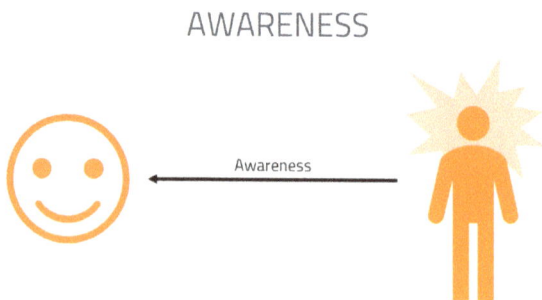

The next subgoal of branding comes further down the branding process, and is here called *relation*. It is essentially about building a relationship with a customer, and to nurture the feelings between that customer and the brand. Here we stumble across the greatest branding question of 2018 and forward: should we use new omnichannel systems (OCS) to do what we used to to do, but more effiently – i.e. create an integrated market communication, where we make sure the brand is manifested the same for everyone? Or should we instead use the power of OCSs together with big data and advanced MA to exploit the new possibilities in developing a more multi-faceted brand personality specialized in unique and individualized consumer relations?

RELATION

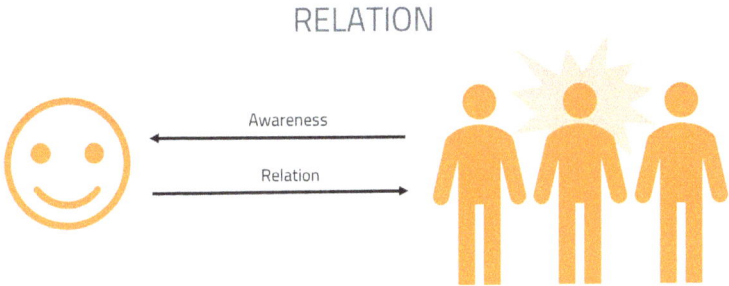

Next in line is the subgoal *community* feeling. We have now progressed from the relation between a brand and a consumer to a social solidarity-like community involving many consumers with emotional ties to the same brand. There is a reason why this is called the "Holy Grail" of marketing, and today's business world is teeming with examples of it. You have success stories such as Sony's PlayStation Community, which is an exceptional example of an online space for gamers to connect; My Starbucks Idea, which is basically a digitalized "suggestion box" but located in a place where all coffee-enthusiasts can connect, interact and discuss their ideas with each other; or Airbnb, which admittedly is community-driven by nature, but no less successful for that reason.

Even such a simple thing as owning an iPhone or a Galaxy these days ignites a feeling of connection with another user of the same phone. There is a subtle, subconscious sense of sharing the same "lifestyle"—and that is the heart and soul of the *community* feeling.

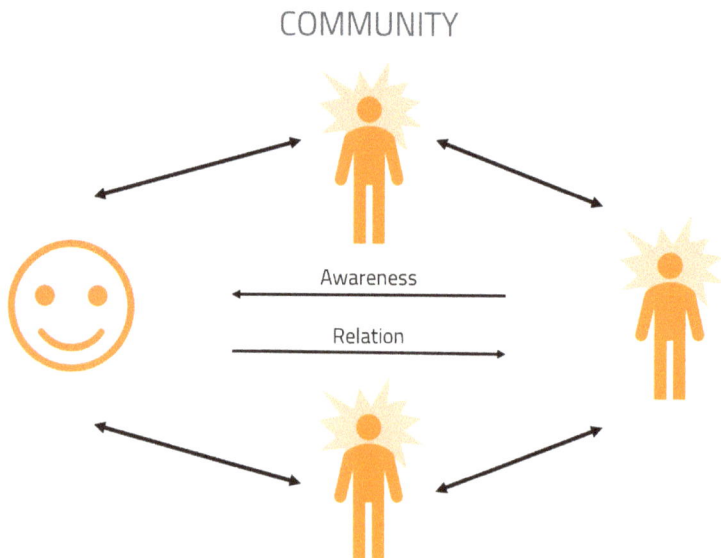

COMMUNITY

Awareness

Relation

The digital excels at stimulating *awareness*, though there are other marketing tools that are about as good at the self-same function (print to some degree, TVC more so). For *relation* however, the digital is more or less incontestable; just take things like interaction, personalization and retargeting. Yet even that pales in comparison to the digital's sovereignty when it comes to *community* feeling. Here, digital marketing is black-belted; the social aspect alone fills such a unique role that the only offline marketing ploy that could even dream of matching it is *highly* frequent events.

After this you will now give the business goal the same treatment as we gave the branding goal—i.e. breaking it down into three separate subgoals. These all relate to various point in the purchasing process—first we want to tempt a new customer to *new sell* (suspect → prospect → customer). Then we want the very same customer to make another purchase via *repeat sell* (a Mercedes-Benz driver buys a new car from the same company when he is upgrading two years later). Lastly, we want to persuade the customer to try our other products (a grocery shopper usually purchasing one particular brand of milk also buys the cottage cheese from the same manufacturer).

DIGITAL GOALS

Strategic goals

Just like we did with the general meta-goals, we will here allocate a 100% between the three branding subgoals and the three business subgoals. The result will be six digital subgoals working together toward the ultimate goal of the digital strategy.

Relationship marketing in three steps

The entire digital branding chain borrows its theory from relationship marketing and the social bond that develops between different individuals.

1. In order for a man to even initiate a relationship with a woman, he must first be aware of this potential partner-to-be's existence (= awareness). But that won't get him far. Nothing will ever happen unless either of the two approach the other to strike up a conversation, show some attraction and hint at what a fantastic future the two of them will share.

2. It isn't until then that the two can start building an intimate relationship, and if not ending up as a one night stand, butkeep dating ina passionate love affairultimately ending with a ring on the finger (= relation).

3. Then things get serious. The couple gets to know each other's friends and families. Suddenly they have a strong social glue binding them together on a level a plain relationship could never match—this is the strongest kind of connection, making it exceedingly difficult for the two to ever separate (= community).

What is the expected result?

And why exactly are we doing all this? Because the six digital subgoals all require their own special treatment, and by figuring out both which are the most important for us and how to prioritize between them this will tell us which means are most suited to address them. That part is what marketers in general deem to be the most difficult part—prioritizing between the five digital marketing means.

But this is the subject of the next chapter.

Digital goals analysis

Identification of what goals to use for the digital campaigns, in order to get a good grip on the development of the entire digital strategy.

1. Start the digital goals analysis by performing a prioritization allocating a 100% between the strategic focuses *branding* and *business.*

2. Within the branding segment, specify further by allocating a 100% between the three subgoals *awareness, relation,* and *community.*

3. Within the business segment, specify further by once again allocating a 100% between the three subgoals *new sell, repeat sell* and *cross sell.*

Multiply the result of 1 by 2 and 3, to get six weighted subgoals (all adding up to 100%) that will rule your choice of means ahead.

Step 3: Means analysis

The motive behind the third step

Even though identifying and specifying goals might very well be the single most important step in the development of a digital strategy, the biggest subsequent challenge is to identify and specify what digital means best address these goals.

In the previous chapter, we examined the five different digital means, their individual trademark qualities as well as their pros and cons. But as already mentioned, it doesn't really matter how good our tools are if they aren't suitable for the task at hand—that is "the specific goal, which the specific company, in its specific situation, wants to achieve with its specific target audiences".

The very first step in this process is to take stock of which of the digital means the company actually has access to. The second step is to examine how well they are doing today (*performance*) in relation to how well they could, and should, be doing (*potential*).

In other words, we have to find out what *investments* in terms of money, systems, human resources and competence have already been made, and weigh that against the *return* they generate. Based on this (historical) foundation, we will know what to *eliminate, consolidate* or *accelerate* in the future.

How do we do this?

In the dream scenario, we can, already at this stage, use big data and especially omnichannel data to evaluate how each respective means contributes to the six branding and business subgoals. For most companies, this is as of yet more of a vision than actual reality. Thus the real matching between our goals and means doesn't happen in this step. What we will be able to take away from this is an estimation of how sizable our investment would have to be in order to take things from where they are today to where they shouldbe tomorrow.

The way to go about doing this is to perform internal or external audits by using various analysis systems to investigate what effect various campaigns in social media, display, search, site and CRM have. This is done in order to find out how "accurately" each digital means is actually performing in comparison to its potential today.

> ### Beware the hidden agenda
>
> Evaluating which means work best for you is important, but there is a dangerous pitfall that you need to be on the lookout for when using external evaluations.
>
> If your company has employed an agency to supply you with, for instance, display or SEM, then obviously they will do everything in their power and more to continue being your supplier. But therein lies the danger.

When the external agency also evaluates how well display/ SEM is doing for your company, it would be crazy to just automatically confide in the results. It happens everyday that major agencies have reported "fantastic results" even though it isn't even close to the truth. Immorality notwithstanding, it is a simple case of self-preservation.

In some extreme cases I've even beheld firsthand how some of worlds' biggest agencies have told almost ten different advertisers how their campaigns have generated the years "record result" on a specific site. Is this just gray-zone sales? Or really unethical conduct? How about downright criminal behavior?

Therefore, always beware of hidden agendas. In fact, it's better to have some sort of unbiased and impartial digital data artist test all results. A good alternative is to frequently perform a 360 degree analysis to evaluate the effects of all digital activities. Control is not mistrust. It is a strategic safety precaution.

The analysis should preferably follow the consumer journey and be divided into traffic-driving and traffic-managing channels. The first treatment goes to the *reactive* portion of the traffic-driving channels, such as social media, display and search. After that we treat the traffic-managing segment, like site, campaign sites, apps, e/m-commerce, etc. Lastly, we take care of the *proactive* parts of traffic-driving channels, like EMM, alerts, SMS, etc.

A digital audit is performed by collecting quantitative input as produced by the company's analysis tool of choice, apart from its own DMP external systems like SiteCatalyst, Google Analytics, Google Adwords, FB-insights, YouTube Analytics, DBM , , etc. The data itself could, e.g. for social media, be things like engagement rate, viral reach or number of retweets. However, since display, SEM and FB ads concern bought media, we have to use ROI metrics for them, such as cost per thousand visible impressions (CPMV), cost per dwell (CPD), CPQ, CPA, etc.

For site, it can be anything from *Bounce rate* and various types of *Activity metrics*, to pure *Conversion* (so-called BAC analysis). And for CRM, EMM and SEO, things like quality traffic and number of conversions (see Chapter 4 for a more thorough breakdown on how to pick the correct metrics for your company, or download DMP app for a simple tool at App Store/Google Play).

The challenge usually lies in finding something to compare against—a benchmark—since analyses-absent comparison points tend to end in pointless data-rambling rants against a backdrop of unanswerable questions like "How long is a piece of rope?". What we are doing here is comparing performance over time, but also measuring against external benchmarks—to the extent that it is possible.

Personally, I am kept decently updated on the latter type of comparisons owing to the vast bedrock of big data accumulated by my a huge number of interactions with various companies over the years. On the other hand, these hundreds of encounters have left me painfully aware of how big of a problem this constitutes for most individual advertisers.

What is the expected result?
The right type of digital audit, using the correct metrics for the comparison between the various digital means (= performance) and the different internal and external benchmarks (= potential), will give us an initial indication of how well each means tends to perform in relation to how well it *should* perform.

Digital means analysis

Identification of which means best address each of our digital goals.

1. Make an initial inventory of the digital means available to your company.

2. Analyze more specifically which traffic-driving channels (e.g. SMM, digital campaigns, search and digital CRM) are at your disposal. Analyze your current situation and what the means can potentially do for your six customized subgoals.

3. Let the traffic-managing means (e.g. site) undergo the same process. Analyze your current situation, examine how you can improve the three most important steps of the consumer journey (bounce, activity, conversion) and how they can affect your six subgoals.

Step 4: Matching
The motive behind the fourth step

We have now identified both the goals of our digital campaign and the means by which we can realize it. In this chapter we will start tinkering with the actual strategy itself, by finding the optimal matching between goals and means.

Lamentably, there is a frightfully high number of preconceptions floating around in this category—most of which are the spawns of salespeople and bloggers who back them up with little to no data. It is also the category most people ask me about.

Over the years, I have studied this subject extensively—both metadata derived from independent sources and my own analyses based on big data from billions upon billions of impressions. Below is the result of these efforts.

How do we do this?

The digital matching process is designed for finding out which means will theoretically be most suitable to reach our chosen goals, and then give an idea of how to allocate resources accordingly.

Therefore, in order to succeed we need to be very clear on both what our digital goals are and to what extent each digital means is capable of achieving them. This overview will tell us which means are optimal for realizing each respective digital subgoal.

So how do we "guess" this? Do we *assume* things? Do we listen to the words and wisdom of salespeople from agencies and system distributors? Do we let the guy with 30 years' experience in the business tell us what to do? Well, although these things play their respective roles in decision making, we want to gain a more objective perspective, and that is not done from hearsay and assumptions. By rooting our decisions in reliable research, big data insights, meta-studies of success stories and established theory, we maximize the possibility of finding the *right* answers for our specific situations.

Below we will examine each means separately and explore what they are actually capable of doing for each specific subgoal.

SOCIAL MEDIA MARKETING

For which digital goals is SMM suitable?

Branding:
Awareness — some contribution
- 63% of young people claim to use social media to stay updated on brands
- 66% of people under 35 years actively get information on brands and products via social media
- 90% of marketers regard SMM as positive for brand awareness

Relationship — some contribution

- 69% of marketers consider SMM effective at making customers loyal
- 37% consider SMM to be the most effective method of creating customer loyalty
- 30% of companies experience increased customer loyalty after becoming active in social media

Community — strong contribution

- 80% of consumers prefer keeping in touch with brands via Facebook

Business:

New sell — strong contribution

- A study by McKinsey shows that SMM influences purchases, regardless of industry, by 26%
- Two-thirds of all recommendations have a direct impact on purchases
- 75% of consumers report that the product descriptions on social channels influence their decision making
- 78% of small businesses recruit a quarter of their new customers through social media
- 70% of B2C-marketers have recruited new customers on Facebook

Repeat sell — strong contribution

- A survey tracking customer attitudes shows that 67% of Twitter users are more inclined to buy brands they are following on Twitter

Cross sell — weak contribution

- There is currently not enough evidence to support whether SMM is good for cross sell

SMM tends to be very good for branding; while relation is not its strongest suit, it is definitely the undisputed king of creating a sense of community. Furthermore, unlike what most people believe, it isn't responsible for too many success stories when it comes to repeat sell, although it is surprisingly good at inciting new sell.

STRATEGIC GOALS FOR SMM

Strategic goals

Branding | Business

Awareness | Relation | Community | New sell | Repeat sell | Cross sell

Due to the thousands of advertisements consumers are exposed to every day, we have begun seeing a steeply growing case of *selective perception*—i.e. consumers subconsciously ignore most new information. Their attention tends to be automatically drawn to only the brands they already know—much in the same way people tend to only listen to the politicians they voted for. The marketer's solution to this is, put simply, an awesome SMM strategy designed to penetrate the media noise by making use of the consumer's friends.

If I live in a place generally known to lodge a more affluent stratum of citizens, my IP address alone is usually responsible for me being exposed to ads for say, more expensive types of cars, than if I lived in a different neighborhood. Which is very strategically logical in terms of sheer ROI of course, since a person of more modest means probably won't buy a high-priced car. However, if I happen to see a friend's post on Facebook saying that the Toyota car he just test-drove is the coolest automobile he has ever had the pleasure to drive; and if another friend posts that she just saw a handsome hunk step out of an elegant red Toyota; well, then my opinion might have been at the very least positively influenced when it comes to Toyota cars… and more importantly, the brand is now on my attention radar. Toyota has managed to penetrate the media noise, and is much more likely to avoid selective perception in its potential consumers in the future. This might sound silly, and most of us are probably not aware of this, or don't want to be aware of it. But it is fact.

This method is one of few ways we can employ to "resurrect corpses"—i.e. reach through to a target audience that would usually not consider our products. It is no easy task to succeed with, but surely one of the smarter ways. When it works.

DISPLAY ADVERTISING

For which digital goals is display advertising suitable?

Branding:
Awareness — strong contribution
- A study shows that display is 9x more effective than TV in creating top-of-mind awareness
- A study shows that mobile ads have contributed to a 54% increase in brand awareness
- A study by Unilever shows that display increases brand awareness by 24%

Relationship & Community — weak contribution
- There is currently not enough evidence to support whether display contributes significantly to relationship and community goals

Business:
New sell — strong contribution
- 29% of marketers report retargeting ads as being the most useful means of getting new customers
- 7% of all new customers in the finance and insurance sectors stem from mobile display

Repeat & Cross Sell — weak contribution
- There is currently not enough evidence to support whether display is good for promoting additional sales

We have previously discussed how the effects of display have drooped as of late, owing largely to information overload, but also that investments in the means have not changed, despite this.

Is this the result of agencies selling us exposure we don't really need? Or does the banner actually have a role to play in the realization of our digital goals? For building relation, it is more or less a lowlife —for that goal there are other tools that are *much* better. To some degree, this applies to repeat sell as well, even though retargeting is arguably pulling its weight there. That being said, display is still doing a good job when it comes to awareness and new sell.

STRATEGIC GOALS FOR DISPLAY ADVERTISEMENT

Strategic goals

Again, "resurrecting corpses" is not an easy task, even with "smart" means, such as SMM—or, in this case, "strong" means, such as display. We can either put out a "carpet of bombs" that go off with a collective bang over a very short period of time, or we can carefully choose a certain number of places and expose our banners there over an extended period of time—and in this regard display is still a very formidable tool. Repetition IS the law of communication; if we ever want to reach through to a new target audience, or successfully launch a new product, there *must* be a certain degree of frequency to our ad exposure if we want the campaign to make any kind of impact at all.

Golden insight #4: Repetition is the law of communication.

SEARCH ENGINE MARKETING

For which digital goals is search suitable?

Branding:
Awareness, Relationship & Community — weak contribution
- There is currently not enough evidence to support whether search contributes to branding goals more effectively than other means, but it is unlikely

Business:
New sell — some contribution
- 85% of retailers consider search to be the most effective method of acquiring new customers
- 89% of customers start their consumer journey in a search engine
- 57% of marketers in B2B claim that SEO generates the most leads

Repeat sell & Cross sell — strong contribution
- 89% of customers start their consumer journey in a search engine
- 13% of marketers regard SEO as the most effective digital marketing strategy to hang on to customers

We learned in the previous chapter just how important search is for especially action-oriented goals, and this also holds true when we apply it to our digital goals. There are studies extolling search's importance for branding and awareness. Most, if not all these studies have had some connection to Google. I have so far never come across an independent and genuinely credible study showing that search is actually better than other means at creating branding in general and awareness in particular. I'm not saying search cannot influence the brand (all manners of communication do), but as digital strategists trying to maximize ROI, we must ask ourselves if it really is the *best* means to succeed with branding. As of yet, we don't have enough evidence to support the case.

Search is, however, indubitably a fantastic tool to drive traffic—particularly qualitative such, where the consumers have come far in the purchasing process and are thus highly likely to convert. In general, this is most true for repeat sell. In much the same way as the situation for display, consumers tend to click most on brands in the SERP they recognize. For high-engagement products and B2B, this behavior though pertains to new sell as well.

STRATEGIC GOALS FOR SEM

Strategic goals

Branding

Business

Awareness

Relation

Community

New sell

Repeat sell

Cross sell

SITE STRATEGY

For which digital goals is site strategy suitable?

Branding:
Awareness & Community — weak contribution

- There is not enough evidence to support whether site contributes to branding goals more effectively than other means, but it is very unlikely
- Adults in the US who want to stay in touch with a brand are 30% more likely to contact the brand through a website rather than Facebook

Business:
New sell — weak contribution

- The probability of selling to a prospect via site is 5–20%

Repeat sell — strong contribution

- The probability of selling to an existing customer via site is 60–70%

Cross sell — strong contribution

- The probability of selling to an existing customer via site is 60–70%
- Sales have been shown to increase with 3% if cross sell products are displayed on the check-out page of e-commerce sites

Site is slightly more multifaceted than other means. As has been previously mentioned, site still often lies at the very heart of the digital ecosystem. For that reason, it usually constitutes a very important part of reaching our digital goals, most often, in the spirit of omnichannel, incorporating one or several of the other marketing means.

Site also has impact in terms of relation and repeat sell for every single customer visiting. By providing comfortable and straightforward navigation, making them "feel at home" on the site, and essentially making sure they like the sub-pages they browse, we take great steps toward aforementioned two goals. If our site is honeycombed with reviews, sharing functions and other community aspects, the means can also affect our community goal.

STRATEGIC GOALS FOR SITE STRATEGY

For new sell, a strong site is indispensable. Seducing a new visitor with relevant content and attractive design is paramount to converting them. Depending a little on our chosen types of products, reeling in new customers on their first visit is actually kind of rare… although putting them off is considerably easier. What it comes down to for this goal is minimizing risks and maximizing possibilities. With so many of our visitors being window shoppers, skipping to and fro between dozens of sites, we need sticky content to both convince them to stay and later return to our site. This is the reason why I strongly advocate for "return frequency" to be the absolutely most important quality metric for site.

It is when it comes to awareness that site isn't necessarily the most important tool anymore. There is little reason to buy expensive traffic and force customers to transport to us (onsite), when there are easier and more cost-efficient ways to do it "out there" (offsite).

DIGITAL CRM

For which digital goals is digital CRM suitable?

Branding:
Awareness — weak contribution
- 41% of marketers consider email to be the best strategy for brand awareness

Relationship — strong contribution
- Adults in the US are twice as likely to sign up for email than Facebook notifications to stay in touch or learn more about a brand
- 48% of consumers prefer communicating with brands via email

Community — weak contribution
- There is currently not enough evidence to determine whether CRM has positive impact on community goals

Business:
New sell — some contribution (for leads)
- 37% consider EMM to be the best strategy to acquire new customers
- Email works almost 40x better toward acquiring new customers than Facebook and Twitter

- Marketers have ranked email as being the most effective method of acquiring new customers

Repeat & Cross sell — strong contribution
- 70% of consumers open emails from companies in order to receive good deals, discounts or coupons
- 56% of marketers consider email as being the most effective method to secure returning customers
- CRM is known to increase customer loyalty with up to 27%
- Every invested dollar has an average return of $40
- A survey by McKinsey shows that emails that include cross sell products have a 20% higher conversion rate

We talked about it in the previous chapter: digital CRM and EMM aren't exactly seen as the sexiest tools to market your things with. But when it comes to ROI, they have been proven to pull their weight and more—time and time again.

STRATEGIC GOALS FOR DIGITAL CRM

Strategic goals

Similar to the situation with site, CRM is probably not going to work out for us when it comes to awareness. Sending generalized digital news letters to many anonymous recipients is an outdated modus operandi, which is likelier to do more harm than good. For the same reason, it isn't usually EMM that comes to mind when one thinks new sell either, even though there are certain situations where it actually might be a viable tool—e.g. buying email addresses and sending to carefully selected target audiences.

Nevertheless, the channel *can* serve as a step in the process of new sell, namely leads generation. There are plenty of "window shopping" consumers out there whose loyalty are fleeting things—these are the people we want to make an impression on, so they think of our site or brand when they are considering making some kind of purchase in the future. The likelihood of this is unfortunately rather slim though. However, if we manage to nail consumers down in our database, we can easily send reminders and proactively chisel away at them until they are ready to make a purchase.

This is all the more important for already existing customers. Digital CRM/EMM is easily the strongest of all our digital tools when it comes to building relation and encouraging repeat sell, and much evidence supports the claim. By both "storing" our consumers in a database and analyzing the big data derived from their digital customer journeys, we have infinite possibilities to personalize content and custom-tailor offers to appeal to each consumer's individual preferences. And by way of doing that we become nice friends bringing valuable "consumer information" instead of annoying peddlers forking out useless "ads".

What is the expected result?

To sum it up, we have five different digital marketing tools and six digital subgoals. In order to match these, we have to take especially the purpose of our campaign into account, but also several other variables. Below is a cheat sheet indicating the individual significance each means has for each goal.

MATCHING DIGITAL GOALS AND MEANS

This is the essence of all things digital strategy. Bear in mind though, that due to the dynamic nature of digital marketing, these are "truths" that to some degree always are subject to change. They might vary for different industries and for companies with different contextual situations (especially brand strength and product engagement have been proven to have strong moderating effects in big data). But on a larger scale these are solid universal guidelines, and here we are truly approaching the core of digital marketing. Simply put: if you haven't understood this, you haven't understood anything.

More specifically, the purpose of the entire digital strategy development is to identify the digital *means* that are most likely to achieve the company's individual *goals,* using the least amount of *resources* in the shortest possible *time.*

Golden insight #5: Optimal Digital Strategy = probability of reaching goals (%) – using the least amount of resources ($) – in the short possible time (h).

The balance between these three strategic components (goals, resources, time) is a precarious thing to be sure, but it is nothing short of essential for the shaping of our strategy. Take for example a company with extremely limited resources (perhaps operating during a vicious recession). Here the resources themselves become the static variable. In that case it might not matter as much if the company doesn't launch a campaign with a 100% probability of success, or if it exceeds the deadline. The question is rather: which of these variables matter most in our specific situation? Do we want a high probability rate, or do we want to it to be finished as soon as possible.

In another scenario, the goals are the most important variable for a company (for instance, during a particularly flourishing economy, or for a growth company). In this case, resources is the malleable variable, and the company is more interested in how to achieve the highest probability of success as quickly as possible. Once again, the key question is whether we regard the probability rate to be more important than the time it takes to execute the strategy, or vice versa. In the next step, this strategic choice of path will then be matched with the investments required for each respective scenario.

Finally, it must once more be stressed that all of the above are strategic *indications*, not bulletproof, universal axioms that hold true for every conceivable situation. That being said, the theory is well-founded in established research, a vast array of surveys, and big data derived from a multitude of both personal and other parties' studies and insights into the development of companies.

"Low Hanging Fruit" first

Some companies choose to overlook what the digital strategy recommends and instead focus on what's "politically possible" or "politically important" within the company.

These types of companies may also choose to implement a "quick fix" that gives short-term results instead of going for a better solution that would give a better ROI in the long run.

On occasion, this might actually be strategically justified, as getting an early "success case" can grant you leverage and get you more support within the organization.

Years and years of working with hundreds of companies in many different contexts and countries have shown how the specific context of a company almost always trumps the "general truths" when we get nitty-gritty on a detailed level. Which means that, in order to achieve a genuinely successful digital strategy for our company, we have to be firmly rooted in the "reality" of our situation. But first, a dose of the Moment of Truth.

Digital matching

Identification of what digital means best suit each digital goal.

a) Use the result from the digital goals and means analyses as the basis for a digital matching.
b) Identify which traffic-driving means best treat the chosen goals using the least effort (= effect on branding/business).
c) Identify which stage of the traffic-managing process (BAC) best treats your chosen goals, using the minimal effort.
d) Rank the digital means by how well they deliver on the various goals.

d) If needed, extend the analysis by performing an internal mapping of already existing digital means and their performance in relation to potential.

e) If needed, perform an external mapping of relevant success stories with different types of digital means.

f) The prioritization of the digital means is performed by analyzing each means' a) pros and cons (return), b) economic and organizational demands (investment), and c) how *a* and *b* interact (return on investment).

g) Perform a matching between the relevance of all digital means and the chosen goals, by allocating 100% between them.

Step 5: Moment of truth
The motive behind the fifth step

So far the strategic process has been largely theoretical, and much of it has concerned what "should" be done according to established theory and big data analyses. In this fifth step—the Moment of Truth—we will root our strategy in the reality of our own respective situations. We will now take a closer look at how and why we generally tend to distribute budget and head-count according to how theory dictates it "should" be.

Using the results of the previous matching as input for the strategic resource planning makes for an exciting dynamic process. Maximizing probability while using the least amount of resources in the shortest possible time is still our focus, but learning how the organization is prioritizing the digital means and budget in relation to what the strategic matching shows to be optimal often comes as something of a… surprise.

How do we do this?

An example of a tried-and-true method is to first try to adapt earlier expense reports to be in accordance with the five digital means. Then do the same thing for all HR resources involved, regardless whether we are talking about headcounts in a large marketing organization or how a specific individual uses his digital hours in a normal work week. These two resource allocations can then be matched with the digital strategy allocation in order to identify dissonances.

This often results in very insightful (and as previously mentioned, usually surprising) clues as to what areas are guilty of wasting resources, even though it might not necessarily constitute a "catastrophe" for the company's budget allocation and organization.

In order to lead the digital campaigns to success, the digital strategy and the digital resources have to be in synchronization. There are basically only two conceivable scenarios here: either 1) we adapt the resources to the digital strategy (outside-in perspective), or 2) we adapt the strategy to the resources (inside-out perspective).

For maximal digital success, the first scenario is obviously preferable. The strategic choice between the two courses of action hinges on things like how much "sunk costs" there has been in earlier investments, systems, partners and organizational development; but actually also where in the company hierarchy the decision-taker in the digital strategy development sits (in general, if this person is high up in the hierarchy, the strategy tends to win; whereas, if he is lower, historical budget and organization usually decides the outcome).

With that said, no strategy is entirely independent of the organization set to implement it, and as such there might be things in the "theoretically optimal strategy" that simply have to be changed or adapted… and sometimes it might even be the wise thing to do. Adapting your strategy to reality will get you better results than sticking with a plan that isn't practical.

This adaption process tends to manifest itself in one of two ways. Either we have the obedient organization that passively adjusts to the new strategy as it is, no questions asked; or we have the engaged organization that creatively "translates" the strategy to fit in with the local context.

The latter scenario usually takes its mighty toll on the person implementing the strategy, but when all is said and done, it generally has a much higher rate of success. By adapting contextually, we reach the sweet spot between theory (strategic work) and practice (operative work). Cherry on top, there is emotional benefit to reap from the organization working together to implement the (presumably successful) strategy.

Golden insight #6: Creative "translation" often gives better results than obedient "implementation".

To sum it up, it can be "difficult" for a person who is not high in the organization hierarchy to completely eliminate historical and organizational obstacles that are not adjusted to the digital strategy. But even though theory claims that strategy has the highest potential to maximize business and brand strength for the company, it isn't necessarily a disaster to alter it, because of the possible benefits of contextual adaption and the internal engagement it engenders.

The word strategy stems from the Greek *strategia*, and even though many people nowadays don't like the connotation, it's hard to get around the fact that it actually means the art of warfare. In Ancient Greece, the general of the army—known as the *strategos*—would effectively stand no chance against the enemy without the army (*stratos*) at his command. Even today, this concept still applies—although obviously in a much less dramatic sense. If your employees don't support the strategy, it will be difficult to succeed with it.

Spillover effects of digital strategies

Have you ever heard of the butterfly effect? That is a little like the spillover effects that sometimes occur in companies.

For instance, implementing a digital strategy might entail consequences that affect other company strategies. These impacts are not always visible to the eye, and it's not unusual that companies are unaware of them.

But spillover effects aren't necessarily negative.

Imagine an example for a global company, that after six months yet not had implemented its digital strategy. During this period, the analog strategy though had absorbed so much inspiration from the digital one that they had almost become synonymous, which had an extremely positive effect on the company.

What is the expected result?

But to really make sure our digital investments turn us into today and tomorrow's winners in terms of both branding and business, we must be both aware of the fact that our actions might need adaption, as well as be prepared to actually do it.

> **Golden insight #7:** It doesn't matter how good our strategy is in theory, if it doesn't work in practice.

What it's all about is using the result from the digital strategy development as the main ingredient in the budget work. We want to utilize our long-term strategic guidelines as input when we shape the digital organization—when we recruit, capacitate and structure our processes. Because it doesn't matter how good our strategy is in theory, if it doesn't work in practice. If we discover dissonances between our strategy and *budget*, there is a number of aspects that need to be analyzed:

1. Have any otherwise low-priority areas been assigned higher budgets as a result of internal or external parties with vested interests?

2. Is obsolete competence in any departments/employees influencing the budget?

3. Do any sunk costs from last year suggest the prioritization of certain different activities?

4. Are external agencies offered discounts good enough to motivate an increased prioritization?

5. Are there any synergies between means from the same distributor that justifies reprioritization?

When uncovering dissonances between strategy and *organization*, there are certain other aspects to consider:

1. Is it possible to capacitate existing employees to fit into the new strategic plan?

2. Is it possible to recruit new employees for the tasks that need to be done?

Moment of truth

Taking stock of what means the budget and organization prioritizes in order to maximize the synchronicity between strategy and resources; aid in the digital campaigns; and avoid wasting resources.

a) Take stock of what resources your budget allows you to use.

b) To the extent that it is possible, try to categorize the budget according to your strategy.

c) Compare the digital means your matching showed should be prioritized in order to reach your goals, to the historical budget of each respective means.

d) If you come across discrepancies between the distribution in your preliminary new strategy and the historical budget, revise the distribution in accordance with the strategy.

e) If your budget incorporates means that do not go well together with your strategy due to e.g. sunk costs from previous campaigns, just bite the bullet and revise the strategy.

f) In the case of e) above, make it clear to the organization that it will very likely influence the realization of the goal.

g) Similarly, take stock of the organizational resources at your disposal.

h) Categorize the competence in headcounts according to your strategy.

i) If the level of competence in the digital organization isn't up to par, consider the possibility of capacitating the employees to ensure a better synchronicity between organization and strategy.

j) If capacitation is not an option, consider the possibility of reorganizing/recruiting new employees to ascertain a stronger execution of the digital strategy.

k) If i)–j) above is not possible, retreat a bit and adapt

the strategy to work with the organizational resources that you actually have at your disposal.

l) In the case of k) above, make it clear to the organization that it will very likely influence the realization of the goal.

m) Compile a final outline of which prioritized digital means, adapted to the available resources in terms of budget and organization, the analysis showed have the highest chance of realizing the company's digital goals.

Step 6: Moment of strategy
The motive behind the sixth step

In the sixth step, the Moment of Strategy, we will take yet another step in the process of adapting our strategies to the practical nature of our individual realities. This we will do by observing priorities and identifying synergies and redundancies with the company's other strategies. What is imperative to keep in mind at this point is that our digital strategy, no matter how great it seems at first glance, will never be successful unless it takes into account the other strategies of the company.

> **Golden insight #8:** It doesn't matter how good your digital strategy is, if it doesn't take into account other strategies in the company.

How do we do this?

This can be done in two ways: partly through manpower and partly through machine power.

Relying fully on "stiff" analyses is seldom the optimal way to adapt the strategy. The first thing we want to do is therefore to organize internal workshops with key employees from each affected department. With the expertise from each respective department brought to bear, we create a highly capable forum where synergies, redundancies, effects, prognoses and competences can be readily discussed. In this manner we will "translate" the general strategy to our local context, just like we talked about earlier; theory becomes practice, general things become specific and—above all else—all digi-strategic connections are adapted to the company's context.

The greatest challenge here usually lies in avoiding inter-political designs and influences. By all means necessary, we want to isolate the discussion to the strategic competence with no ulterior motives.And the potentially vested inter-ests of internal politics are not the only pitfalls either—even worse is the risk external parties entail (e.g. agencies, IT con-sultants, system distributors, etc.).

As the strategic work progresses, these workshops tend to spawn a million questions, and possibly more. Amid these are (at least) six that are absolutely obligatory though. These six questions will focus on the contextual conditions that might influence individual means' "theoretical" impact (both posi-tive and negative) on different digital goals.

1. Analyze whether any of the low-priority means have such synergy with high-priority means that they should be boosted.

2. Analyze whether any of the low-priority means have such synergy with offline means that they should be boosted.

3. Evaluate whether any of the high-priority means have such high synergy with other means that both should be boosted.

4. Delineate potential redundancies between your priori-tized means that might justify the decreasing of one of them.

5. Examine whether any of the high-priority means require

so much budget or time that they might have to be decreased.

6. Analyze whether there is such good internal competence in the company that any of the low-priority means should be boosted.

But any digital strategist worth his salt doesn't just make do with manpower to ensure the fruition of the strategy though; by employing the powers of analytics, we crank the probability of success up significantly. Performing scenario analyses to test how different combinations of digital means affect the digital goals, has been proven to be highly valuable in this regard.

This method doesn't provide 100% scientific answers, but it provides solid indications as to which direction to keep moving in. It also works like a learning tool. This is the point where the "moment of strategy" really happens for most people. It is also the point where the digital strategy finally assumes its ultimate shape.

What is the expected result?

In the first dimension we use *man power* to examine the relative effects of each respective means, and in light of the conclusions made we revise the strategy accordingly.

In the second dimension we utilize *machine power* to calibrate the digital strategy further, by running scenario analyses.

Moment of strategy

Synchronization with other strategies, e.g. by identifying synergies and redundancies between other means, both online and offline.

a) Examine whether the selected means require too big of a cut from the budget or time allocation to succeed, and if it might be wiser to strike them from this year's budget and reconsider them next year. Or if they—with regards to lead time—quite contrarily must be initiated immediately.

b) Analyze whether there are other means apart from the selected ones that should be included in the strategy on the sole qualification that they have such strong synergy with any of the already prioritized means.

c) Evaluate whether some of the selected means should be more prioritized due to potential synergies.

d) Evaluate whether there are any previously discarded means that have such high synergy with important offline means that they should be included in the digital framework.

e) Delineate potential redundancies between the selected means in order to evaluate whether it is possible to remove or reduce certain means and thereby optimize the budget.

f) Evaluate whether there are means that have been discarded even though there is such high internal competence that they might actually yield higher results than the initial analysis suggested.

g) Analyze the causality between the various means, e.g. if the effect of a certain means hinges on that of another and should for instance be scheduled earlier from a sheer developmental point of view.

h) Perform workshops with concerned parties (ideally ones without vested interests), where the results from the previous steps Matching and the Moment of Truth confront the results of the Moment of Strategy.

i) When the final result has been filtered through human brains, use it as input when performing scenario analyses to test against the selected goals.

j) Compile a summarization of the selected means and their expected results (given optimal execution).

Step 7: Digital roadmap
The motive behind the seventh step

We have now finally managed to generate a real digital strategy, inspired by both established theory and big data. We have rooted the strategy in our company's individual reality by letting it go toe-to-toe with budget, organization and already existing strategies.

But strategy is considered to be abstract in nature by many people (and some might even venture as far as saying "fuzzy"), and to some extent, this is true. In order for strategy to actually leverage change, a final step has to be taken, and it is arguably the hardest—we have to go from thought to action. In order to turn expectation to realization and fiction to fact, we have to translate a set of very general goals and means to a concrete, localized roadmap.

Because unfortunate though it may be, it doesn't matter how promising the digital strategy is unless it corresponds to a set of concrete actions.

> **Golden insight #9:** It doesn't matter how good your strategy is, if it doesn't translate to concrete action.

How do we do this?

And for that reason, in the seventh step we will translate all our previous strategic work to something practical. We will set concrete activities in a "transformational roadmap" with milestones, meta-goals, subgoals, etc. This roadmap can have many faces, but once more there are six fundamental cornerstones that should never be disregarded.

DIGITAL SCORECARD
The first part is designing a custom scorecard guaranteeing that all activities are means to the same end. The scorecard also ensures the maximal efficiency of all activities, not just for each respective means (unichannel), but also when it comes to the relations between different means (omnichannel).

EXPECTATIONS AND REALIZATION

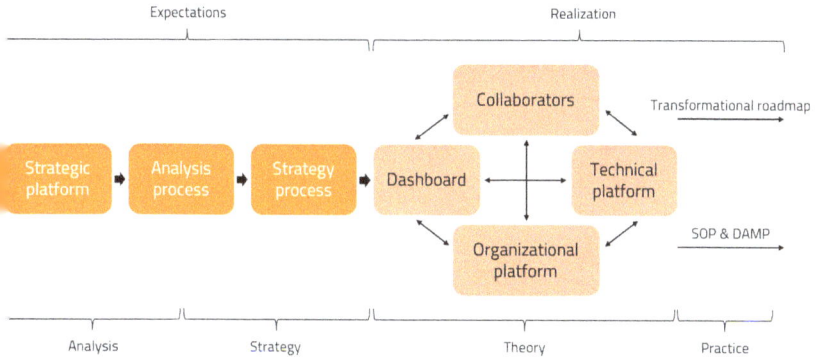

It is the possibilities of measurement which digital marketing entails that make it possible for internal and external parties to both work successfully toward digital goals, as well as make sure their efforts are directed toward the results that the KPIs measure, and not the results the KPIs are measured against. (We will take a closer look at the process of creating scorecards in Chapter 4).

DIGITAL ORGANIZATION

The second part is developing the organizational platform—recruiting, reorganizing, restructuring processes, capacitating, etc. Again, it might seem strange to adapt the organization to the strategy, but that is actually not the case—the very word organization derives from the Greek word *organon*, which means tool. So, in sheer theoretical terms, the organization is a tool meant to realize the strategy and achieve the goals the company has set.

Still, as aforementioned, no strategy is completely independent of the organization set to carry it out. The degree to which the organization should adapt is contingent on things like company ambitions, budget and perspective. There are less appealing things to consider here, such as internal politics, but also dynamic aspects like engagement, enthusiasm and job satisfaction that can be used as fuel to optimally reach the goals. (In Chapter 5 we will closer examine things to consider during the digital transformation of an organization).

DIGITAL PARTNERS

The third part is the selection of collaborators for the implementation and realization of the strategy, such as the development of our already existing agencies and system distributors; recruitment of entirely new suppliers of the "traditional" variety (communications bureaus, media agencies, etc.); or enrolling suppliers of the "new" digital variety (DSP distributors, contemizers, conversion professionals, digital auditors, Marketing Automation vendors, omnichannel suppliers, etc.).

Historically, outsourcing plays a large role in the marketing world, and selecting and developing network partners is of paramount importance. Making the right kind of demands when it comes to briefs, processes and follow-up controls is one of the most strategically important aspects for a marketer

in this regard. Another is to make perfectly clear to any external parties that we as marketers have the final word when it
comes to the digital goals and strategy. Preferably, outsourcing should be kept to a minimum, and when it is necessary
it should be solely reserved for issues of a more tactical and
operational nature, as long as they live up to the stipulated
KPIs.

Risk of Dependency

Relying too much on external agencies can come to spell
trouble. Not all of them might share your motivation and
dedication to your company, simply because… they are
not part of it.

The incident below, is an example of something that
actually happens very often in the world of marketing:

A content agency was employed to post an ad about a
competition on Facebook. The total extent of this agency's
efforts involved copying and pasting the client's email
verbatim, and then posting it on Facebook.

And when they did, they even managed to include some
of the email instructions that were meant for the agency's
eyes only. And to add insult to injury, they also charged
compensation for several hours for their "work".

It just goes to show that you need to be careful when
dealing with external companies. They might not know
your company, your market, or your customers the way
you do, or in the worst case scenario—they might not
even care.

DIGITAL TECHNOLOGY

As soon as the digital strategy has been translated into KPIs, and both internal and external partners have been chosen, time has come to venture into the world of digital platforms. These are the tools with which the organization and partners will realize the strategy, and range from CMS's, email systems and CRM databases and DMP for owned media, to SMM analysis tracking, adserving for bought media and full-scale omnichannel systems with big data and marketing automation.

Whatever the choice though, it is important that these pieces of the puzzle are added *after* the strategy is hammered out in its entirety. We should never allow technology to determine what is possible and what is not. Instead, we should choose the systems that are most likely to realize the full potential of our strategy.

DIGITAL IMPLEMENTATION

The first four steps of our roadmap—the implementation of a scorecard, organization, partners and technology—are tactical building blocks to enable us to see our strategy through to fruition. Now it is time to start considering how exactly this will work in practice.

One of the most sure-fire ways to proceed with the digital transformation is to create a transformational roadmap with universal focus areas divided into action points (APs), which in turn are organized into both the RACI model (Responsible – Accountable – Consulted – Informed) and the Gant chart. Post-transformation, experience has proven it successful to have processes organized according to a standard operating procedure (SOP), in combination with responsibility allotment according to the RACI model and a Gantt schedule for the timelines of the projects and elements of the strategy.

TRANSFORMATIONAL ROADMAP

Transformational roadmap

Activity	March	April	May	June	July	Aug
Display			▇			
Capacitation for digital campaigns			▇			
Campaign process				▇		
Implementation of campaign					▇	▇
Digital CRM						
Analysis of results					▇	
Overview of EMM system						
Evaluation of EMM system						
Implementation new EMM system						▇
Social media						
Capacitation						
Conceptualization					▇	
Potential experimentation						▇
Analysis of possibilities						

DIGITAL OPTIMIZATION

Lastly, we reach digital optimization. In combination with the intrinsic possibilities of measurement and interactivity digital marketing entails, it might arguably be one of the foremost hallmarks of the trade.

Being able to continually evaluate and optimize (analysis & action) is THE key success factor to maximizing ROI during the entirety of the development process. Here this process isdubbed DAMP, which stands for Digital Agile Marketing Process, and it incorporates everything from retargeting and DCO of display, AB/MV-testing and conversion optimization of site; to SEO and SEM optimization and content optimization for EMM/SMM etc. Or in other words, an omnichannel-inspired big data solution based on data-driven insights via seamless interaction in all possible digital touchpoints, independent of inhibiting aspects such as departments, budgets, distributors, etc.

What is the expected result?

The end result of these six steps is the translation of our strategy to a tangible roadmap. We have now taken the step from theory to practice, and we have done it in a way that maximizes the probability of success, using the least amount of resources and in the shortest possible time.

Digital roadmap

Translation of our selected goals and means to a tangible roadmap in order to make sure our digital campaigns of the future will be successful.

a) Translate the final version of the strategy into the discrete activities necessary to ensure its successful realization.

b) Develop a customized scorecard to ensure all involved parts work toward the same goal in as efficient a manner as possible.

c) Outline the organizational platform necessary for the implementation.

d) Examine and define which collaborators are needed for a strategically sound execution.

e) Investigate what type of technical platform is required.

f) Outline a plan for the implementation, development of the scorecard, organization, required technology and potential recruitment of agencies.

g) Decide on a platform for the agile evaluation and optimization required to maximize ROI for the full development process.

Summary

We have now been enlightened on how a sound digital strategy can hatch from the 7-step process, a tried-and-true methodology that includes specification of both goals and means as well as a subsequent matching of them, followed by an adaption to other strategies, organization and budget.

In Step 1 we took a much-needed step backward to assess our own background, our customers, our market and our already existing business and branding strategies.In Step 2— possibly the most important one in the entire process—we specified what our digital goals were, first for business and branding and then for various points in the customer journey.In Step 3 we mapped out what means are available to us.In Step 4 we reached the core of the strategy—the matching between the goals and the means.

In Step 5 we moved our strategy one step closer to reality by comparing how we allocate between budget and organization in reality, and how theory dictates we "should" do it.In Step 6 we took a second step in the same direction, and rooted our strategy in practical reality by identifying synergies and redundancies with other strategies the company might have. In Step 7 we finalized our leap from theory to practice by translating our strategy into a series of concrete activities in a digital roadmap with milestones, meta-goals, subgoals etc.

The final result is a comprehensive digital strategy which has the highest possibility of helping us reach our goals using the least amount of resources in the shortest possible time.

CHAPTER 4:
DIGITAL AUDITS

What will we learn? *The importance of having full access to credible data, and how to specify appropriate KPIs for digital scorecards.*

Why is this important? *To ensure that the digital strategy is executed correctly, and to maximize ROI during the entirety of the process.*

The last two chapters have been pretty clear on one thing: the digital strategy is completely crucial to maximizing ROI in digital campaigns. Nevertheless, together these initial chapters constitute but one of three vital conditions for digital success.

This chapter, focusing on the second of these conditions, turns the focus to the immense possibilities of digital auditing which digital marketing enables. The subsequent chapter will treat the third condition, namely the value of the digital organization charged with the task of actually doing the job.

This journey begins with us learning how the accessibility to data can help us with primarily three things: control, optimization and insights. Thereafter, we will learn how to identify and specify appropriate and viable KPIs for the digital scorecard relevant to our own particular company, using a simple 4-step process and a 3-dimensional reference sheet.

By way of doing this we will not only ensure the correct execution of our digital strategy, but also learn how to maximize ROI in our digital campaigns by controlling, optimizing and analyzing our efforts.

The digital background
The myth of complex digital audits – status: debunked

In recent years, I have hosted a large number of seminars, workshops and lectures, many of which were based on the theme of digital audits and their contribution to digital success. Some of the questions that typically has popped up during these seminars were: How do I do this? Do I base my metrics on effects or ROI? Is there any value in web analysis, or is MV-testing the way to go? Is it necessary to deep-dive into the ocean of big data, or is a simple digital scorecard enough to assume control of my digital marketing?

In this chapter we will take a closer look at the insights that were birthed during dialogue with a huge set of marketers regarding digital KPI:s. We will find that as a marketing director, there is absolutely no need to be at the mercy of analytic consultants and number-crunching staff members. Instead, we will learn how to easily take control of our digital marketing, keep track of how it's doing, and monitor how both employees and agencies perform in relation to potential. That digital marketing and sales audits must be highly analytically complex is a myth we unceremoniously put to an end.

Of marketing problems galore

It should be no mystery to us at this point that the digital is the most crucial subject for marketers at any company—whether they know it or not. This holds true in both local and global contexts.

And as such, the most tender question of this chapter is: where exactly does the modern marketer turn for trustworthy answers to these and similar questions?

THE MARKETER'S MANY QUESTIONS

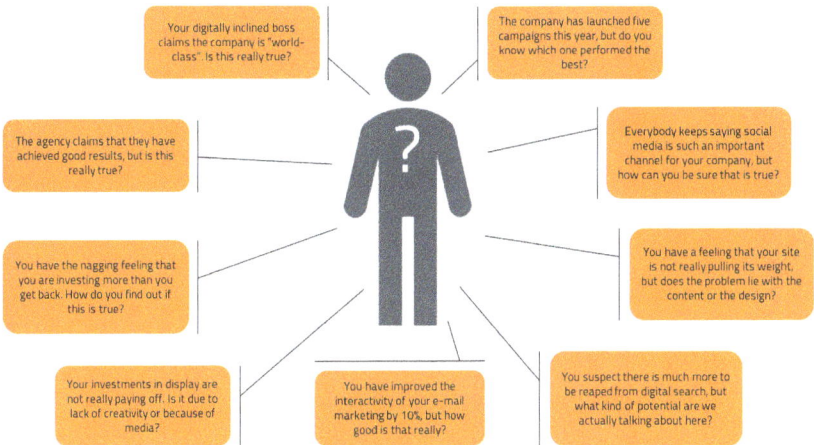

Your digitally inclined boss claims the company is "world-class". Is this really true?

The company has launched five campaigns this year, but do you know which one performed the best?

The agency claims that they have achieved good results, but is this really true?

Everybody keeps saying social media is such an important channel for your company, but how can you be sure that is true?

You have the nagging feeling that you are investing more than you get back. How do you find out if this is true?

You have a feeling that your site is not really pulling its weight, but does the problem lie with the content or the design?

Your investments in display are not really paying off. Is it due to lack of creativity or because of media?

You have improved the interactivity of your e-mail marketing by 10%, but how good is that really?

You suspect there is much more to be reaped from digital search, but what kind of potential are we actually talking about here?

Digital audits – four promises

The solution to all our woes spells digital audits. As DMS is in a state of what could quite aptly be called pubescently rampant growth, the importance of control, optimization and insights—as made possible by digital audits—grows accordingly.

If we had been working exclusively with analog means, the answers to aforementioned questions might have been based on personal experiences, qualitative judgment garnered from some study or the average result of what a few individuals in a focus group report. When working with digital media though, the answers we derive from digital audits are uncompromisingly "true".

In this chapter we will examine how this actually works in practice, and my promises to you as digital commander-in-chief are these:

1. This data is more than readily available to you as a marketer.

2. This is the most reliable data there is.

3. If done properly, performing digital audits is a breeze.

4. Used correctly, the digital audit is, along with general digi-strategic knowledge, the very essence of digital success for a modern marketer.

Above all else, digital audits are significantly easier to carry out than people usually think. They require about five times as little time and understanding as is generally purported, and definitely results in return, reliability and digital success ten times higher than the investment made. What it's all about is using the digital scorecard as guidance for the strategy, and not the operative handiwork performed by web analysts and digital marketers in their day-to-day work.

Therefore, this is a chapter for those in charge of the digital marketing, as well as the people aspiring to become such—people who are generally highly pressed for time and who need to make quick yet sound decisions. Or people who are not averse to using straightforward tools and moderately easy means to turn themselves into digital heroes at their companies.

Digital conditions
Trust me – I'm a digital audit

With digital audits we lead the process so far away from the old biased routines of the marketing industry that the whole thing begins to take on the characteristics of science. Interrogating people to deduce their attitude when it comes to brands and products is hardly an effective means of collecting data, and thankfully the practice can now be considered gone with the wind. We are not limited to what people "think" they will choose, consume or buy anymore—now the quantifiable digital behaviors of our targeted consumers generate super-strong indications of what they *will* choose, consume or buy.

So: sporadic questionnaires or focus group surveys allegedly "representing" all other target audiences. Or behavioral research with a 100% population penetration and 100% answering frequency. How about the latter?

The power of this cannot be stressed enough; a case where analog attitude surveys beat digital behavior research is practically nonexistent. Data-driven insights not only turn us wise beyond our years—it also provides concrete results. In other words, digital audits pave the way for digital success.

There's more where that came from

There is such a vast abundance of tools to aid your digital audits that you will have no problems finding one to your liking. The usual suspects when it comes to *offsite* systems are Facebook Insights, Adform, Mediamind, Flashtalking and DoubleClick for campaigns; Adwords for search; the SMM and EMM systems' own analysis tools for SMM/EMM, etc. For *onsite* systems, Google Analytics and SiteCatalyst are all the rage, while Optimizely and Test & Target are good candidates for AB/MV-testing. Omnichannel systems, of course, are in a league of their own; systems like Adobe, Eloqua, Salesforce, Hubspot, et al. bring analysis to a whole new level.

The qualitative difference between these systems tends to vary quite a lot, especially where onsite systems are concerned, although third party systems are generally known to be guilty in this regard as well. That being said, contemporary systems usually keep a high enough level of quality, whether we are talking about data or the processing of it.

The difference in the generation of KPIs comes down to ownership. Who owns the system (usually third-party, licensing it to second-party or you as first-party)? Who owns the data (usually you, even though second-party has been given the right to collect and process it)? Who will have access to the data (practically always you, although it depends a little on what kind of contract you sign with the agencies—however, in accordance with all ethic guidelines you SHOULD have full transparency in your media purchases, so unless you get full access to the audit system, your contract is… highly dubitable)?

By assuming control of the system itself (by demanding access from third party/buying it ourselves), we have come a long way toward ensuring great results in DMS. If this turns out to be too much of a hassle, the second-best option is to at least assume control of the data, which, both legally and ethically, belongs to us as first-party.

With this done, we have officially taken our first step toward using digital audits as a tool to reach digital success.

The three purposes of digital audits

So, the data of digital audits is very reliable. And the systems are highly available. How about its alleged simplicity in terms of usage? Before delving deeper into that matter, we will first look to the three different purposes a digital audit can have.

As seen in previous chapters, digital marketing has flushed across the world of marketing like a tidal wave, and most things analog is disappearing with the ebbing waters. Digital marketing is crowning itself king, and the reasons are primarily three: firstly—and perhaps most obviously—consumers are migrating to the digital realms, and advertisers have little choice but to follow.

Secondly—though not any less importantly—digital marketing possesses an innate interactivity rendering it unrivaled as a marketing communication medium. One of the prime characteristics of this is the fact that while analog media is inextricably built on *monologs*, the interactive functionalities of digital media promote *dialogs*. This turns digital marketing communications dynamic beyond comparison, and substitutes the exanimate information reaped from analog media with the very much human interaction originating from digital media.

Thirdly, the unparalleled, and next to unlimited possibilities of discretely measuring this human interaction is something no other channel can even dream of matching.

Three different functions

There are primarily three different purposes to digital audits. The first is *digital control*—perhaps the most obvious one, and (unfortunately) the most widely used.

The second function is for *digital optimization*. Optimization arguably makes the largest operative difference for companies, since it not only permits more human-like and relevant dialogic interaction between the marketer and consumer, but also maximizes ROI and the positive impact on branding and business.

The third function—*digital insights*—embodies what might very well be the most strategically important aspect for companies seeking to conquer other market areas and become stronger competitive forces.

Three different roles

If we take our digital auditing endeavor to *control* but no further, our efforts will be comprised of merely rather simple analyses that can be conducted by an accountant. We will glimpse backward in time and use historical data to measure our performance in relation to potential. We might uncover everything from *dos*, *maybes* and *don'ts,* to immediately actionable knowledge.

By using digital auditing for *optimization*, we choose the path of the modern marketer. We will look at contemporary results that might give rise to just as simple conclusions as in the first function, although we will here compare the results from two roughly equivalent entities (a banner, post, site header, pic, clip, etc.) in order to determine which alternative is the most eligible.

Employing digital audits for *insights*, however, is something else entirely. We will now assume the role of the strategist and turn a weather eye to the future. The accountant in the first function wants to learn why things have or haven't worked in the past. The marketer in the second function is interested in why one certain entity performs better than another, knowledge he subsequently uses to maximize ROI. In this third function we want to identify patterns and elucidate key success factors (KSFs) to devise tailor-made policies, SOPs and strategies which will help us increase our competitiveness on the market and our strategic triumphs in the future.

Three levels of complexity in relation to results

The first function—digital control—is straightforward enough and boils down to identifying and analyzing KPIs. The second function—digital optimization—is actually also reasonably elementary, and revolves around specifying and comparing the KPIs of different but comparable entities (such as AB/MV-testing, retargeting, DCO, etc.).

The third function—digital insights—is considerably more advanced and can get rather complicated. In theory, it could be as easy as forwarding a specific issue you are contemplating to an external/internal web analyst or a digital data artist. It can get so complex though, that we find ourselves standing in the middle of a major strategic crossroads where our choice of path is decided by big data. All that is collected from several different data sources and processed in advanced statistical analyses, as well as cross-indexed with both primary and secondary data.

PREREQUISITES, INVESTMENT AND RETURN FOR THREE DIFFERENT PURPOSES AND MEASURMENTS

Prerequisites			Investment	Return
Purpose	Focus	Role	Complexity	Success
Control	Past	Accountant	⬇	➡
Optimization	Present	Marketer	➡	⬆
Insight	Future	Strategist	⬆	⬆

If our goal is to attain digital success, the third function might not always be the way to go; using the very simple means in function one can already result in fantastic digital control of our digital efforts, irrespective of how many channels we operate in, how many partners we contract and how sizable our investments are. Likewise, by using the equally simple means of function two, we can increase our ROI not with 10, 20 or 30% over a few years, but with up to 100, 200 or even 300% over the same time span.

This doesn't in any way reduce the value of strategic insights, but if ours is not a high-level, global multibillion company focusing heavily on DMS, engaging the third function might not always be necessary.

We will get extremely far using function one for gaining control and function two for optimization—the first one ensures that our efforts are on point, while the second boosts our results. Curiously enough, they are both fundamentally the same though—all that differs is the mode of execution. The reason is that digital audits with results from days past, and digital optimization concerning how best to maximize efforts in the present tense, both stem from the same digital KPIs—KPIs that are preferably gathered in a digital scorecard. As stated, the difference lies in the application, not the origin, or even "perspective".

The accountant develops KPIs by analyzing the past. She might find "white spots" she considers to be lousy situations that could have been handled much better, and she might direct the blame to substandard staff performance either internally and/or externally. The modern marketer looks at the exact same KPIs, but sees a golden opportunity for improvement instead.

Below we will go over how these KPIs are constructed, and then follow a simple 4-step process to identify what digital KPIs are best suited for our own individual companies.

The digital solution
The tools for performing digital audits are plenty and the results are reliable. The two functions we have selected are easy to use, but they still enable great digital success. Now all we need is to understand how to do a digital audit in practical terms.

In order to do this, we will first expand a little on how the process of creating digital KPIs works, before embarking on the 4-step journey to identify digital KPIs that are localized to each individual company.

The structure of digital KPIs

We are well aware of the digital audit's reliability at this point. We know what systems to turn to. We have control over our data. We know that focusing our fire on digital control and optimization yields great results with relatively small complexity. But how do we structure the KPIs necessary for all this?

We will now engross ourselves in the actual construction of KPIs. More specifically, we will consider the differences in various KPIs based on effect, relevance, the consumer process, channel and function.

KPIs based on effect

The framework of digital KPIs consists of two vital components, the first of which concerns the achieved effect (return), and the second the investment made in terms of resources (investment).

When we measure the effect of our digital investments, knowing whether we are focusing on *quality* or *quantity* is key. The effect can take the shape of absolute numbers (e.g. 10 million inscreen impressions during the latest campaign, 10,000 visits on our site, etc.). A healthy matrimony between this and *trends* of absolute numbers (e.g. year-on-year (YOY)) is often necessary to steer clear of seasonal influences and similar aspects that might skew the results. Furthermore, the effect can also be measured by effectiveness (e.g. 2% dwell rate on an exposure, 1% CVR on traffic).

Media agencies don't optimize

About a year ago I came across the discouraging report that some of the world's largest media agencies still use "impressions" as their main performance indicator for display. Big wonder measurement and analysis fall between the cracks… and not to mention optimization, being of such laborious nature that it actually requires a little effort to pull off.

The two dimensions quantity and quality are by no means mutually exclusive; quite on the contrary, they work best in symbiosis.

If we learn that our direct traffic is of top quality in terms of e.g. CVR, it doesn't matter so much if we also know that the direct traffic in quantitative terms hasn't yet reached its full traffic potential. Instead it might be the search traffic, which incidentally has the highest volume in absolute numbers, that has the highest growth potential in terms of conversion maximization.

Using qualitative metrics exclusively may even generate misleading results.

The pitfalls of inaccurate KPIs

A mainstream metric for search is nowadays "share of total traffic"… which is disastrous in the sense that it can give potentially skewed and biased results. Using optimization, we have the ability to alter the numerator (search traffic in absolute numbers), but not the denominator (total traffic that may be dependent on campaigns, seasons, demand and so on). In plainer words, if we heroically boosted SEO-traffic with 10% one month, while the total traffic, due to a massive campaign, increased by 50%, it will look as if we failed with the SEO… even though SEO actually did increase with 10%.

Another lopsided metric some companies use is measuring the activity on a site using page views/visits. In this case, a conscious effort to promote horizontal traffic directly leading to the conversion page (= higher likelihood of high CVR) would suddenly indicate lower success than the convoluted obstacle course vertically leading traffic through numerous transit routes before reaching the conversion page (= lower likelihood of high CVR).

An even more common practice, though no less ignorant, is focusing on CTR in newsletters. This results in the same type of suboptimization. Imagine, for instance, a month/department that sends a newsletter to 10,000 subscribers with a popular product that gets a 10% CTR. This will indicate higher success than a month/department that sent out a total of three different newsletters: one to 8000 subscribers with a CTR of 12%; one to 7000 subscribers with an 8% CTR; and one to 10,000 users with a 5% CTR. More specifically, it will look as if the latter generated -20% effect, even though it has resulted in +100% more interactions.

Using qualitative metrics with caution is therefore recommended. Using them in combination with quantitative metrics even more so. In some cases, even exclusively using quantitative metrics is warranted—after all, in the previous three examples, we are interested in the increase in search traffic in the first one; the increase in quality traffic or number of conversions in the second; and the number of interactions with our customers in the third one.

In whichever case, we are *only* interested in what effects the digital activities have generated. And since we don't want the analysis to grind to a halt in pointless discussions about "how long a rope is", these measurements are often accompanied by comparison over time or with internal/external benchmarks.

KPIs based on relevance

But this is just the beginning. The realm of effect metrics abounds with options, but I have already made a promise about simplicity. Because the thing is, performing digital audits is not about raking together as much information as possible—it is about acquiring information as *relevant* as possible.

What with the immeasurable amount of available digital data, it is an easy thing to lose yourself completely in all the options and go crazy with metrics and analyses. But that is not what this book is about. Our perspective here is that of the busy yet modern and ambitious marketing directors, in dire need of quick and easy access to relevant data in their efforts to control and optimize the digital campaigns being performed by coworkers/agencies/partners.

The objective is identifying and specifying a few KPIs that are as relevant to the digital result as possible (there is a reason, after all, why it is called "Key Performance Indicator"—we would rather have one or a few keys to a single door, not two dozen).

KPIs based on the consumer process

We can divide our effect metrics into both direct goals such as sales (offline) and indirect goals, such as "top of mind", "NPS" and "preference", etc., which are measured in attitude studies of a more abstract nature. Direct digital goals we know to impact indirect goals are also relevant here.

As a first step in matching metrics and goals, we can take a page out of the digital strategy process in Chapter 3 and use business and branding as the fundamental basis for our KPIs. How much has our digital activities contributed to the first segment of the branding process *awareness*—i.e. a light acquaintance with the brand? How much has it contributed to the second segment, where we start building a *relation* with the target audience? How conducive has it been toward forging a sense of social *community* for the entire customer base?

In the same manner, we will look at the three business sub-goals. How have our digital efforts bolstered *new sell*? Have they helped extend customer relations with *repeat sell* and/or *cross sell*?

KPIs based on channel

Digital audits offer a tremendous level of both reliability and validity compared to analogously measuring attitudes based on random "representatives", but we are talking about a virtual ocean of different metrics to keep track of.

The world organization in online marketing, IAB, which I founded in Sweden a few years ago, has made great contributions in this field by standardizing various metrics for especially media sites and bought media. They still have a way to go though. After all, the internet is a dynamic medium unlike any other and is capricious to say the least; new channels come and go all the time. Add to that the global titans in social media that have grown so large that they can practically set their own standards, and it's even more of a moving target.

Because of this, the comparability between different channels isn't always fully reliable. For that reason, it might be wise to differentiate between channels and not use "identical" metrics so much as "similar" ones. For instance, how exactly does a page view on a fan page relate to a page view on a website? How strong of an indication of engagement is dwellrate on a banner as compared to likes on FB or retweets on Twitter? What is the relative value of dwelltime in the interaction with a banner compared to session time on the site? In all these cases there are similar metrics but no identical ones—thus it might be prudent to not blur the lines between different channels too much.

KPIs based on focus

So far, we have looked at metrics gauging the "effect" (return) of our digital efforts. The second component of ensuring a true ROI:al marketing campaign is investment. Investment is typically easier to quantify since it usually concerns money, although it also includes things like invested time, head-counts, consulting services, etc. Which, of course, by extension also concerns money.

For practically all owned and earned media, effect metrics are usually enough, although they can, on occasion, be combined with the odd time metric. When it comes to bought media though, we must always account for the investment made, i.e. combining what we *get* (return) with what we *give* (investment). The result is a ROI metric for control and optimization of our bought digital activities.

The amalgamated metrics embodying both return *and* investment tend to take two different shapes, although the industry traditionally focuses chiefly on only one. You could say that we have inherited it straight from the analog world. The metric in question is cost/benefit, where our investments are the numerator and the effects gained are the denominator (cost/benefit).

This metric is a good type of metric if the goal is to minimize resources, i.e. if we want to pay as little as possible for the end value.

POSITIVE DEVELOPMENT OF ROI VS. COST/BENEFIT

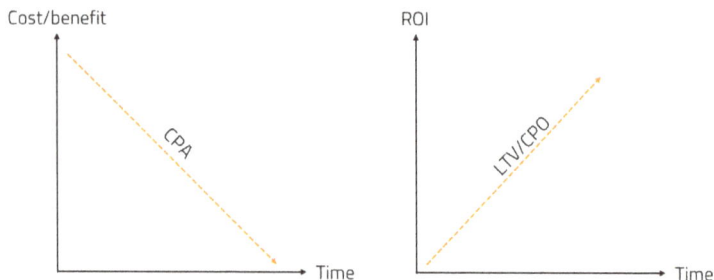

Some of the more modern metrics are of a considerably more ROI:al nature, even though the almost silly difference is that our gain (return) now ascends to the numerator and our investment drops down to the denominator. Basically, we get an inversion of cost/benefit, but with the slightly more inspiring challenge of maximizing the effect. We simply want to get better pay (return) for our work (investment).

In a sheer psychological sense, cost/benefit metrics are superb for companies struggling with survival, or for markets shackled by recession. ROI metrics are more functional for companies with growth goals and when the market economy is flourishing. The analog media world has seemingly run aground in a sterile expense-minimizing mindset, like CPM, CPMV, CPC, CPA, etc. (see branding metrics below). As more modern applications for the digital world, we are starting to see the embryos of more virile tools like LTV/CPO etc. (see business metrics below).

KPIs based on function
KPIs can be divided according to their function as well, i.e. whether they are used for control or optimization. In the latter case, by optimizing the customer experience by continuously adapting to the quickly evolving market. With the aid of high-end statistical methods like AB/MV-testing and OBA we simply leap past the "insights" segment, test things in real-time and then choose the option that best maximizes the effect (and, somewhat non-nostalgically, we completely disregard why).

Again, common practice in this regard is dividing the KPIs between business and branding. In an *attribution analysis* we look at how the interaction between different channels induce a certain action from a consumer, whereupon we use view-through metrics to identify what contribution a specific channel's exposures have had toward conversion in another time and another digital channel.

In a *digital campaign optimization (DCO) analysis*, we identify what customers, channels and creatives are the most contributory in digital campaigns, and then remove the underperforming ones. This entails the obvious advantage of being able to analyze and maximize the effect while the campaign is still active—not afterwards, when it is too late.

With *site optimization*, we shift our attention from analyzing traffic-driving activities (offsite) to traffic-managing ones (onsite). Here we take steps like streamlining the journey customers will take, refining the user experience (UX) and editing design and functions in order to attune the branding experience for customers until it's as good as it possibly can be.

Content optimization is essentially the same practice, although—as its name might lead one to realize—we now optimize the content. This involves identifying what manner of structure, type and length the content should optimally have, or what nature of pics and clips tend to attract or deter customers—both when it comes to the general aspects of "one size fits all" as well as personalization (1-2-1).

Conversion optimization includes both site and content optimization. Usually it focuses on one or a few of the funnels through which customers reach the point of conversion, such as purchase, app download or newsletter registration.

In a *retargeting analysis*, we examine what manner of creatives are most effective at attracting return visitors, and/or shepherding them further in the purchasing or branding process.

A modern marketer spearheading a company that is using all these methods can be said to be part of a *Digital Agile Marketing Process* (DAMP). The distinction is that, unlike in analog media, where the workflow is often *think→ do→ analyze,* we embark on an iterative process of "Analysis & Action". Through a kind of analytical "dialogue" with the customer, we can identify what manner of interaction and communication is attractive enough for consumers to bite.

And the result isn't "just" substantially increased customer attraction, but also an equally strong growth in ROI. With correct execution, we are talking 50–100% increased effect… or more. So $2 million is suddenly $4 million, and $10 million is suddenly $20 million.

This isn't something a responsible marketing director should do tomorrow. It should be done yesterday.

Golden insight #10: The definition of insanity is doing the same thing over and over and expecting a different result.

Most people are aware of the particular nugget of wisdom that Einstein allegedly imparted on us, yet such an amazing number of marketers and agencies insistently do that exact thing. If a marketer does the very same thing over and over, every day, every week, every month… why then would he also expect to improve his results? This is why digital auditing for digital optimization is so important in order to succeed. Without it, how would we know any better than just continuing our obsolete (and potentially disastrously ineffective) investments and campaigns?

But if we use digital audits, we make sure we are not the inadvertent victims of aforementioned scenario. On the firm foundation of a number of digital KPIs, we do things differently and consequently also get different results (read digital success). To make matters even better, we are not talking about rocket science here; we are basically using the very same KPIs as we did for the first digital auditing function control.

The actual difference concerns the level of analysis more than the metrics themselves. When optimizing, it is crucial that we measure the effect disparity in at least two digital versions (e.g. posts, creatives or images) of things that have identical prerequisites (e.g. that are on the same site or in an identical location, of identical design and from the same time span).

This is why both control and optimization—both "accountant" and "marketer", if you will—use the same metrics (e.g. CTR or CVR) even though the scrutiny differs (e.g. aggregated for a certain campaign or site vs ceteris paribus for a simple creative or web text).

Identifying digital KPIs

After an introduction to how reliable digital audits are, and how accessible the tools and systems used to perform them are, we selected two functions which are relatively easy to use but have the power to greatly influence our future success. After that we overviewed the structure of digital KPIs by examining the selection and construction of effect metrics and their relevance. We also inspected four ways to organize our digital KPIs, based on the purchasing process, the channel, ownership and functionality.

But how exactly do we select specific KPIs that are relevant to our individual companies and our most important digital goals? Below we will delve into the generic prerequisites that apply to everyone, before employing a simple 4-step process to identify our own digital KPIs. Lastly, we will discuss a few practical implications.

Generic prerequisites

Apart from any technical aspects—like the ability to perform the measurement of the metrics, and access to reliable data—there are five specific prerequisites instrumental to the composition of strong digital KPIs:

1. They must, as comprehensively as possible, describe the digital *success criteria* of the main goal.

2. To the extent that it is possible, they must exist within the actual *capability scope* of the *developing* party.

3. They must be *explicit* and *straightforward* with as little room for interpretation as possible.

4. They must be *datable* and avoid any lag effects.

5. They must be *actionable* and not only of "analytically" interesting nature.

As dictated by SMART—Specific, Measurable, Achievable, Realistic, Timely—our goals must also be realistically achievable. For a marketing director though, the most important insight is that these five goals are not entirely compatible with each other.

Focus on action

A digital audit is always comprised of at least two of these three steps:

1. *Analysis:* The first step of the analysis is always processing the data and chiseling out concrete digital results. This initial step gives an indication of what has happened, and in its unpolished form it provides groundwork for audits and control at best, although it usually only whets the appetite to do and find out more.

2. *Insight:* In this second phase the questions take on a more intellectually interesting tone—now we find out why something has happened. This is where wisdom stems from. The data-driven insights as generated from the analysis coalesce as the foundation for learning.

3. *Action:* There is nevertheless no digital analysis or data-driven insight that serves a full purpose on its own; they are only relevant if we can turn them into some kind of

beneficial action. In the first case—analysis—we derive an estimation as to whether something has worked well or not. For instance, something that has worked poorly in the past might be tweaked in order to work well in the future. Or perhaps our findings indicate that one thing has previously worked better than something else—in which case we might decide to do more of the former rather than the latter. The second case—insight—provides us with the knowledge we need to develop viable and successful strategies, policies, processes and partnerships, as well as make other strategically relevant choices.

The third step is the most significant one when it comes to digital data. The focus of all analyses and insights is therefore the action that must eventuate. The digital world has seen many years pass since it was strategically justified to use web analysts and digital data artists to amass mountains of "reports" for the sole sake of reporting.

The concrete 4-step process – a digital cheat sheet

Now that we have specified the generic prerequisites in general and the focus on concrete action in particular, we have finally gotten to the point where we can start identifying the digital KPIs that are relevant for each of our individual companies. The process starts with an overview of how digital KPIs are constructed:

1. **Goal:** For which digital goal is the KPI supposed to be? Within branding: awareness, relation or community; and in business: new sell, repeat sell or cross sell?

2. **Channel:** Which digital means will we control or optimize? Social media, display, search, site, CRM? All of them?

3. **Control:** Are we talking bought or owned media? We will be using ROI metrics for bought media and effect metrics for owned media, preferably in combination with absolute numbers denoting quantity and performance metrics for quality.

4. **Function:** What function does our digital audit fill: control or, optimization? Will we analyze on an aggregated level or on a ceteris paribus level?

After having addressed these four criteria, we can now select a suitable KPI by consulting the 3-dimensional cheat sheet of digital KPIs in the image below.

4 STEP PROCESS FOR THE DEVELOPMENT OF DIGITAL KPIs

	Awareness	Relation	Community	New sell	Repeat sell	Cross sell
SMM	Bought: CPI, (like, CPI) Owned: Organic reach	Bought: CPT (talking, favorites, etc) Owned: Fans, followers, likes, pins, interaction rate	Bought: CPVR (viral) Owned: Sharing, retweets, viral spread	Bought: LTV/CPO, CPL, CPA, CPO Owned: Revenue from SMM, leads from SMM, etc.	Owned: Revenue from SMM, orders from SMM, repeat sell from SMM	Owned: Quality traffic from link to product offers/services/sales
Display	Bought: CPM, CPMV	Bought: CPO, CPI, CPC, CPQV	Bought: Viral spread/investment	Bought: LTV/CPO, CPL, CPA, CPO (non-logged in)	Bought: CPO (logged in), retargeting CPO	Bought: CPO (logged in), retargeting CPO
Search	Bought: CPM Owned: New visit to site from SEO	Bought: CPC, CPQV Owned: Quality traffic from SEO	Bought: CPA sharing Owned: # sharing from SEO	Bought: LTV/CPO/SEM Owned: New traffic to site, conversion level search traffic, SEO sales	Bought: CPO SEM (logged in) Owned: SEO sales	Bought: CPO SEM (logged in) Owned: SEO sales (logged in)
Site	Owned: Total traffic, direct traffic, new visits	Owned: Session time, page views, return visit frequency, site registrations, logins	Owned: Reviews, quota and number sharing, community activity, comments on blog posts, logins	Owned: Degree of conversion, new sell, new leads	Owned: Number of orders per customer and month/year/life, orders from logged-in mode, share logged-in	Owned: Number of products/orders, repeat sell, share logged-in mode, cross-traffic on site
CRM	Bought: Bought contacts Owned: Total contacts/month, contact/member/month	Owned: Number of active members, quality traffic to site, CTR	Owned: Viral spread, traffic from sendouts in community campaigns	Bought: CPA, CPL, CPO from bought contacts Owned: New members in DB	Owned: Sales from sendouts	Owned: Click/interaction with cross sell material/sendout, cross sell from directed sendouts

For example, if the company's 1) goal is to create awareness through 2) display, there is a wide array of appropriate KPIs like impressions, inscreen impressions, dwell rate, interaction rate, CPM, CPMV, CPD, CPI, etc. Then, if it is 3), the effect of the bought media we are looking for, the choice is either CPMV or CPD, depending a little on our level of ambition. Is 4) the function then optimization and not control, our final KPI is CPD per channel/placement/format.

The key here is the fact that it is actually very simple to extract a KPI that is just right. Surveilling and acting on these chosen KPIs gives us all the requisites we need for digital success.

Practical application

Identifying and selecting our KPIs is half the job, and the important half at that, but we still have some work left to do.

As previously mentioned, a KPI in and of itself doesn't do much unless it is acted on. This action requires people, and for them to understand we need to give our scorecards a logical and easily followed structure. Preferably, the scorecards have a dashboard where the users can easily understand the connections between various KPIs. The people who need or want to know more have easy access to the indications underlying the KPIs (preferably in hyperview).

For the people who are not as enamored of numbers, having a scorecard with easy and quick indications might be a good idea too—e.g. green and red flags, traffic lights, etc. After developing the digital scorecards, there are also four additional paths of more individual nature:

1. With what *frequency* will it be sent out?

2. To *whom* should the scorecard be distributed?

3. Should different people have different *access* to the scorecard?

4. What *predefined action* should be assigned to each person and *KPI?*

Number 4 is especially important when it comes to the optimization function. It is advantageous to have an itemized SOP with measures to take depending on the various outcomes of the KPIs. To the extent that it is possible, avoiding the "human factor" is paramount to realizing the full potential of digital scorecards.

All of these things are still within the scope of what busy marketing directors can keep track of. With a few simple means, they can get control over their companies' digital campaigns and success, and thus become digital heroes.

To reach yet another level, we have a fifth practical challenge: finding a clever way to accumulate all the digital data from the scorecards into a digital cyclopedia in order to discern trends and follow the development as it progresses. That way, we can not only control and optimize, but also start identifying patterns to generate insights, which will eventually help set our bearing on a more strategical level.

We are now approaching the next step of digital auditing—data-driven *insights* and all things digital big data—but more on that a little later.

Summary

Unlike the answers we get from analog studies—attitudes and opinions at best—digital audits bestow on us scientific results based on quantifiable digital behaviors. Digital auditing also enables real-time monitoring with 100% answering frequency on 100% of the digital population. The bottom line is, data harnessed from digital audits is extremely *reliable* data.

Digital audits require different systems for measuring, usually divided between offsite and onsite systems. If we are using a digital auditing system for our digital activities, we are in most countries by law entitled to access, and sometimes ownership rights, to both the data and the system. Here the bottom line is that digital audit data is highly *available* data.

There are three different functions in digital audits that promote digital success: control, optimization and insights. The first function concerns the past and its complexity is low; the second function concerns the present and is just slightly more complex than the previous one; and the third function concerns the future and is highly complex. However, as long as we focus on the first two functions, digital audits provide great results and are still easy to perform.

With the 3-dimensional cheat sheet for the selection of digital KPIs, we can identify what KPIs are most optimal for our specific situations. This selection is performed in four steps:

1. Which digital *goal* will it relate to?

2. Which *channel* do we want to control or optimize?

3. Does the digital activity concern *bought* or *owned media*?

4. What is the *function* of the digital audit?

After the digital KPIs have been chosen, we need a digital scorecard to transform our plan into practical steps. After that, we address these four questions:

1. With what *frequency* will it be sent out?

2. To *whom* should the scorecard be distributed?

3. Should different people have different *access* to the scorecard?

4. What *predefined action* should be assigned to each person and KPI?

Armed with a comprehensive digital strategy and a digital scorecard, we are now ready to set our bearing for maximal digital success. There is yet one potential snag in our grand schemes though.

They walk. They talk. They make *mistakes.* We call them humans.

.

CHAPTER 5: THE DIGITAL TRANSFORMATION

What will we learn? *The reasons behind the digital paradigm shift and the revolutionizing consequences of the digital transformation.*
Why is this important? *To make sure the company implementing and carrying out the digital strategy takes important organizational questions into consideration.*

With a sound digital strategy in our pocket and an adapted digital scorecard, we have come well on our way to digital success. You might not have noticed, but the latter is actually the first step on the transformational roadmap succeeding the conclusion of the digital strategy chapter. The next step is overviewing the multitude of processes, profiles, structures and cultures that are part of the organization set to realize the full potential of the digital strategy. Therefore, we will now go over a number of organizationally crucial points to take into consideration when implementing a digital strategy.

Initially we will explore what *the three biggest reasons* are for the digital paradigm shift, from disruptive communication technologies for freedom-fighting consumers to digital commercialization. Thereafter we will discuss *the digital transformation's momentous consequences* for society, industries, companies and individuals. all done in order to avoid our digital strategies becoming theoretical paper tigers.

The third phase of the digital revolution

It is becoming more and more evident that the digital revolution is entering its third phase. After merely being an *digital experiment* that grew to become a *digital trend* for a select few, the *digital tsunami* has now drowned us all completely. Whether we like it or not, the digital is now a cardinal part of the daily lives of most of Planet Earth's inhabitants, companies and countries. In this third phase, the revolution no longer only immerses certain generations (digital natives), departments (digital departments) and countries (digital divide), but everyone, everywhere, all the time.

The only path leading to the digital top, for talents and companies alike, is to proactively incorporate the digital in every aspect of the company, into the continuous capacitation of individual employees, into the very DNA of the company's culture and structure. Because the thing is, around us rages a paradigm shift the like of which Earth has never experienced before, and it will have revolutionizing impact on the life of every human, company, industry and country. The old trend word for this paradigm shift is *The Digital Transformation.*

The dialectic triangle of disruptive technology

Popular belief is that new technology underlies these changes. First the technology "came" (being in this case something abstract in the sense that it "came" all by itself), whereupon everything had to be adapted to it in some sort of deterministic linear process.

And obviously, such is not the case. Just like the Berlin Wall didn't "fall" in 1989 (it was a highly social process, brought about by people in very specific social contexts), this technology didn't just "come". Contrarily, it has been incrementally brought into being by an exceedingly social process, which has grown to be as the result of the interaction between a huge lot of people in various social contexts. Instead of looking at the technology like a linear process formed by logic, it should be regarded as a circular process formed by dialectic.

If we look at this from a bird's eye view, the first tendencies of change stem from what could be described as a "freedom war" that took place while the previous millennium ticked to its conclusion.

THE DIALECTIC TRIANGLE OF DISRUPTIVE TECHNOLOGY

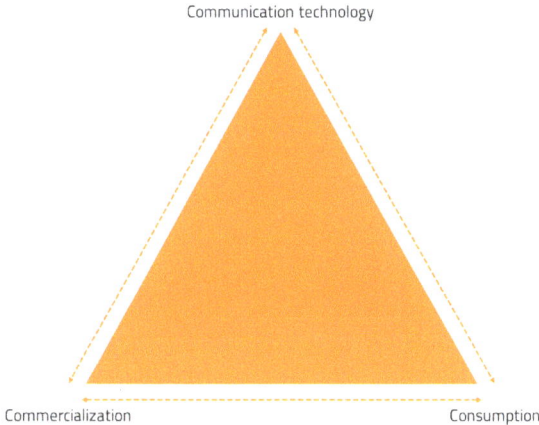

Communication technology

Commercialization   Consumption

We can envision this dialectic relationship as a triangle between research and development of *communication* technology in one corner, rampant expansion in freedom-hungering *consumption* in the other, and intra-/entrepreneurial forces in *commercialization* in the third. Below we will address each of these in turn.

The disruptive communication technology

Of course, the development of technology plays a highly central role in all of this. The many passionate scientists and researchers developing the technology that is used for both consumption and commercialization are in no way negligible. Yet a chain is only as strong as its weakest link, and while technology comprises a necessary premise in the context, it is a necessary but not sufficient premise..

Take for instance the internet itself: from the conception of ARPANET by scientists in 1969, via the creation of the World Wide Web in 1990, to the first search engines in 1994 and iOS and Android in 2007 and 2008. Communication has undergone a similar journey, as connectivity progressed from modem to broadband and then to mobile broadband and mobile hotspots. Then there's the hardware: we went from large computers to personal computers; then to laptops, tablets, smartphones and smart-TV; then to Google Glasses, Galaxy Gear ,, HoloLens and Magic Leap; and soon to digital lenses and retinas, Kurzweilian implants, etc.

Whether we are talking about the evolution of hardware, connectivity or the internet, the digital technology has, by itself, played a central role. Of course.

But it has never seen the job done by itself.

The freedom-hungering consumers

The argumentative bottom line we finally reach is that technology by itself is not enough. Science sociology reveals an endless array of technological innovations that never took off, despite equally "revolutionizing" potential. Research indicates that it is a highly social process, and not just the actual development of the technology—but also the consumption of it.

In a way, the catalyst can be traced all the way back to the fall of the Berlin Wall. Because just like the people of Eastern Europe refused to accept the *structural* shackles their dictators forced upon them, the people in the Western World decided to break free from their *cultural* c bonds, different though they were. Top-down communication and information distributed on a need-2-know basis led people to raise their voices in cries for change; fed up with the small group of people at the top using their access to information as a weapon to shut the people at the bottom out.

And suddenly the Western World underwent a transformation. Need-2-know took larger and larger steps to becoming transparent information; top-down communication became bottom-up communication. In some places, this metamorphosis happened very gradually and cautiously, and in other places it was borderline anarchy. With emails, the employee on the floor could theoretically communicate directly with the CEO. With Napster, everyone could listen to whatever they wanted to listen to. Websites improved the transparency for both companies and countries. Social media, in turn, almost completely liquefied the illusionary borders that divided the world, not the least of which were those in the private sphere.

INDUSTRIAL SOCIETY

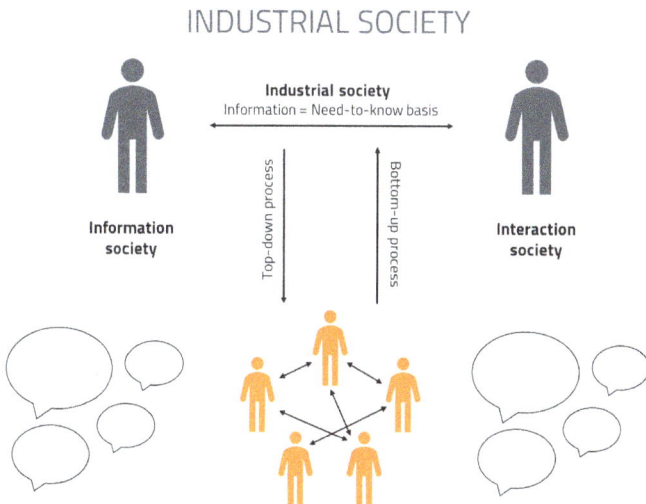

Industrial society
Information = Need-to-know basis

Top-down process

Bottom-up process

Information society

Interaction society

This process has seen us go from nonlinear communication to nonlinear consumer behavior. We communicate digitally, we date digitally, we interact digitally; we talk, read and play digitally; we work, shop and learn digitally—the digital is such an obvious part of our lives at this point that we take it for granted, anddon't even notice its presence.

The filter bubble is all-consuming, and as the world is going totally from offline to online, we can soon start listing the things we are *not* doing digitally instead. Work out, eat, walk, cuddle, have sex. But who knows what the future holds? Soon we might be doing these things digitally as well -with the way things are looking, it's hard to imagine why we wouldn't(even though we might not know *how* just yet).

That all this has dramatically influenced the way we work and consume media is easy to see… and those who can't see will simply have to accept the consequences. And consider themselves outsailed both where business and career are concerned.

The digital commercialization

Despite the fiery passion of technology scientists, and the significant power of a radically altered consumer behavior, it is not enough. We are all part of a capitalistic society whether we like it or not, and thus the fuel for all development and research is money. Generally, researching technology is no cheap task, and neither is developing it.

For the selfsame reason, a third social force is the commercial. Because in the tumultuous midst of all these scientists and engineers burning for technological advancements, and consumers thirsting for freedom in their consumption of information and communication, we have the digital intra-/ entrepreneurs of small and large companies alike—people who ache to bridge the gap between technology and what freedom-thirsty consumers want.

For a short while, the digital expansion lost some of its luster at the turn of the millennium, but it soon came back with a vengeance and drowned us in an ocean of miscellaneous applications and services. More and more digital companies started showing up on the radar—everything from e-commerces to media sites. Platform-owning titans like Mark Zuckerberg, Jeff Bezos, Larry Page, Sergey Brin and co seemed to pop up everywhere; followed by even more socially revolutionizing peer-to-peer (P2P) services based in the sharing economy like Uber and Airbnb. The digital hardware distributors have not failed to keep up either—here we have traditionalists like Dell and Asus in the computer sector, and modern giants like Samsung and Apple with the smartphone, tablet and wearable flagships.

This is the threefold dynamo that is driving the digital revolution around us. The continuous dialectic between communication, consumption and commerce is orchestrating our collective ingress into a digital future, and at this point it has accumulated so much momentum that no man, woman or child can stop it.

The consequences for society

An OECD study shows that practically all young people in most countries are now using the internet. In some countries such as Norway, Netherlands and Iceland the penetration is so total that literally 100% of 16–24 year-olds are estimated to be World Wide Web users. With numbers like that, it doesn't exactly take a big leap of the imagination to predict where online and digital are going in the years to come. This emerging paradigm shift is the result of the previously mentioned symbiosis between freedom-thirsting consumers, disruptive communication technology and a digital commercialization as spearheaded by ambitious entrepreneurs. Together they are invoking a "creative destruction" of entire industries, and—actually—the whole world. The commercial forces are thrusting the whole planet toward a digital tipping point.

Just like the 19th-century *industrial society* started transmuting into an *information society* in the beginning of the 20th century, we are now leaving the latter behind in lieu of an *interaction society*. Consequently, people are no longer passive recipients—we progress from backward information to forward communication; from passive top-down processes to active bottom-up processes. People shun traditional linear TV and embrace circular digital media.

Using new technology to repair old processes is a methodology gone with the wind; now we are instead using new technologies to innovate entirely new processes. Once more the mobile phone proves its competence. The global smartphone penetration has now soared past 50%… and it is giving birth to new processes aplenty as it goes.

The consequences that entail for society are staggering. Simply put, we are talking about a Digital transformation, preferably spelled with capital letters.

The consequences for industries

And it is not just societies and countries that are affected by this; the digital revolution has, and is having, just as large an impact on industries. After we saw the first clickable banner back in 1994, the commercial web on this side of the millennial shift has ensnared, disrupted and ultimately subdued industry after industry, and market after market.

Some of the earliest digitalized areas were ticket sales and services with light digitalized products and low need for offline representation (such as the travel industry, dating industry, gaming and betting industries, finance industry, media industry, etc.). Soon the consumers' mass emigration from the offline "real" world to the virtual online realm forced several other consumer-based industries (like the automotive, groceries and home electronics industries) to invest heavily in digitalization. This didn't only extend to their marketing and sales, but in many cases the companies had to consider complete reappraisals of their value propositions.

There are currently over 4 billion internet users worldwide, and the number of mobile subscriptions has way surpassed the 5 billion mark. Companies nowadays have all the reason in the world to attempt to lead this digital process as opposed to holding off. For a long time, traditional industries—populated by colossal dinosaurs hampered by the sunk costs of expensive retail chains and with offline entities locked by intellectual property laws—tied themselves into knots trying to halt the evolution of the digital.

But the consumers are seldom content with what they have, and their incessant demands for new things has, along with technology research and digital entrepreneurs, driven things forward anyway. This has quite understandably dealt a deadly blow to the old dinosaurs that have been unable to keep up with the inexorable forward movement. The concept is called creative destruction.

One of the more recent victims was the music industry, which Spotify—armed with disruptive technology, digital distribution and innovative business models—made embarrassingly short work of. Meanwhile, Uber is giving the taxi industry a run for its money, Airbnb is challenging the lodging industry and Skype and WhatsApp and WeChat is having its way with the entire telecom industry. The list could go on: not too long ago, Google annihilated the Yellow Pages; Facebook and YouTube have irreversibly changed the media industry as we know it; Wikipedia has unceremoniously dethroned traditional encyclopedias; websites like Hotels.com have ruthlessly propelled the hotel industry into *survival of the fittest*-mode; Amazon once took a large chunk out of the book industry and is together with Alibaba still eating away at it to this day. 1940:s

We can go even further back. Back when VHS smashed Hollywood's monopoly to bits and pieces, and Gates checkmated the large-scale computers. This has been going on for a long time. And who is next in line? The guillotine just might smash down on your industry next. It is *do or die* question. Again it comes down to this question: are we just going to sit idly by while the digitalization changes the world, or are we going to take charge and not only be a digital native in the virtual realms of this brave new world, but also actually lead it?

The consequences for companies

We will now dig a little deeper into what this means in terms of consequences for companies. Our first topic up for debate is the need for a total, uncompromising *transformation*; secondly we will explore what this means for our *interaction* with consumers; thirdly we will treat the consequences for *organizations*; and finally we will examine the ramifications for individual people.

Transformation

First things first: the consequences will be—and are already— tremendous. If we want to own the future instead of just being part of it, we must "transform while we perform"—i.e. we must reshape our companies into something that both streamlines and innovates at the same time. Leading the digital evolution, as opposed to just living with it, doesn't just require the addition of a couple of bullet points on the agenda, but a very restructuring of the company's DNA.

> **Golden insight #11:** If we want to own the future instead of just being part of it, we must "transform while we perform".

The first question is therefore whether we prefer to lead by the *use* of digital instead of surviving *despite* the digital. When it comes to this question, it is my personal experience that the digital often serves as a "trigger to change", inciting the complete restructuring of processes to make sure they fit in with the new digital communication technology. And this has worked because the choice has been to lead by *using* the digital.

But with the digital transformation currently at work, this won't be enough anymore. It won't cut it to just renovate the organization of a company—at this point it will basically have to be revolutionized. And it isn't just the structure that needs reforming; the basic principles and values of the company—its very culture—must be reshaped in the light of the digital transformation.

Golden insight #12: Leading the digital evolution, as opposed to just living with it, requires a restructuring of the company's very DNA.

In accordance with a healthy outside-in perspective, the *very first thing* we look at when contemplating this transformation is our interaction and communication with our consumers. Thereafter, we move on to the organization set to do the job, before narrowing our focus to the individual competence of the talent the organization consists of.

Communication

Communicating with consumers is extremely different today than just a few years ago… and it is so different from a decade ago that there barely is any point comparing at all. In the beginning of this millennium, only a small portion of the marketing pie was digital. In 2016, the global digital advertising spend hovered close to $200 billion, and by 2020 it is estimated to reach $335 billion.

Much of our communication used to be bought media, but today a larger and larger part of it is earned and even more so owned.

Golden insight #13: "Marketing in the future is like sex—only the losers will have to pay for it."

Communication was originally designed prior to a campaign and then evaluated when all was said and done. Nowadays "the finishing line is the starting line", and we systematically design and evaluate over and over again in a constant, agile digital optimization process spanning the entirety of the campaign's lifetime (DAMP).

Golden insight #14: The finishing line is the starting line.

A completely acceptable MI achievement used to be performing the occasional attitude study to find out what a couple of thousand people "thought" their opinions were. The data that we now have real-time access to returns the "real" opinions and behavior of millions upon millions of people. This level of big data has never before been seen.

The communicative activities used to be completely under the marketer's control. Now though, nothing is "under control"; any given campaign might be abruptly and unexpectedly subjected to the viral effect, which can be a two-way street.

Teams used to contain creators who both designed the communication content and made their own judgment calls on the outcome. These days, teams are fortified with digital strategists, digital data artists, programmers and other miscellaneous people—a colorful mélange of internal and external parties.

Suffice it to say, the marketer's world is very different from what it used to be. So are the organizations, the processes and the competence required for success. First came the *sites*,, where traditional marketers took their brochures and flyers and uploaded them, hoping they would be a little cooler just because they were digital. Then came the search engines, taking their place as the first traffic-drivers of the Web, and suddenly we had scaled another rung on the ladder—we went from site to *search*. Then the social revolution took us by storm, and we moved from search to *social*. And now, finally—with the vast prevalence of the smartphone today,

the AR-glasses tomorrow—we are going from social to *smart*.

THE TRANSFORMATION OF INTERACTION FROM SITE TO SMART

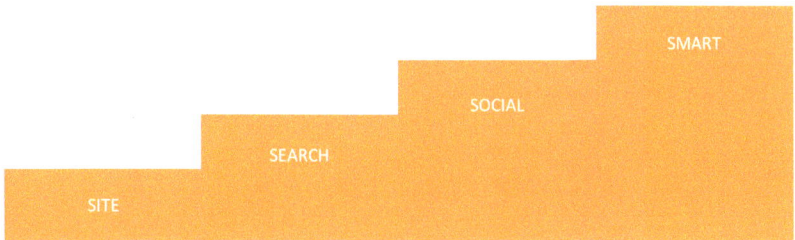

This *site→search→social→smart* evolution has happened staggeringly fast. But that which grows quickly tends to run the risk of ripping at the seams. The solution to this is a digital strategy that holds it all together.

Organization

With communication so strikingly transfigured, with a need for such a different set of tools and with a brand-new demand for competence, it doesn't exactly come as a surprise that the organization needs to be changed as well.

With a growing cast of digital talents, it is only natural

that we organize ourselves into virtual networks, or "cells" as some of the new pioneer companies call it. To stay afloat in this sea of changes we need cross-functional teams that are well-versed in all things agile. We must change our processes (which become integrated), our structures (which turn into networks), our communication (which becomes digital), our recruitment (which becomes flexible), our capacitation (which becomes continuous), our cultures (which becomes receptive), our leadership (which becomes coaching), our technology (which is turned future-safe), our development (which becomes agile), our business models (which become dynamic) and our strategies (which become elastic).

There is an overwhelming number of facets to keep track of, many new terms to memorize, lots to think about and even more to rethink. However, all of this can be readily summarized under the umbrella term *propencity-for-change*—a subject I wrote Sweden's first scientific treatise on at the dawn of this millennium.

We need cultures, structures, processes, leaders and employees that not only have the required inclination to change, but that also have the necessary conditions to make change possible. We need *elastic* competence, technology, business models, strategies and leadership. And, lastly, we need digital communication and distribution.

The only way to survive the digital transformation is integrating all of this into the very DNA of the organization. And if we do, we won't only survive—we'll *thrive*.

The consequences for individuals

Regardless whether we are talking about personal qualifications or learned competence, the consequences for individuals will be enormous. Because just like a large part of the reasons behind the digital revolution is human, so too are the consequences—human.

The digital qualifications

In the years to come, traditional characteristics such as having *Relevant* competence and being *Responsible* are going to be far from everything that will be asked of employees. As our organizational networks grow larger and larger, the social aspect will also start becoming more important (*Relational*). But above all, considering the pace at which our society is changing, the demand for dynamic attributes in both leaders and employees will just increase and increase and increase.

10 RE-CEPIES FOR DIGITAL RE-CRUITMENT

10 RE-CEPIES

1. Relevant
2. Responsible
3. Relational
4. Reactive
5. Receptive
6. Revealing
7. Rethinking
8. Revolutionary
9. Reflecting
10. Recycling

After having recruited and worked intimately with more than 5.000 people in dousins of digital ventures, as well as coaching and interacting with at least as many digitally responsibly people in the hundreds of billion-dollar-companies I've worked with all over the world, I today have ten *Re-cepies for Digital Re-cruitment* that I look for in potential co-workers. A Winner of Today must first and foremost be able to react quickly to change (*Reactive*); be highly *Receptive* to new insights and impressions; dare to divulge everything he or she has found in this digital world of transparency (*Revealing*); be able to find a balance between completely *Rethinking* processes and achieving *Revolutionary* things on one side, and *Reflecting* on what already works (*Recycling*) on the other.

Life-long learning

The key difference still lies in *competence* though. Gone are the days when we spent a lot of time learning and then a lot of time working. "Long" educations still live on as platforms, even though shorter and more practical ones are on the rise.

But long or short, there is sadly no hope of either being enough. *Lifelong learning* is the only path that leads to the future. It has gotten so far already that anyone who wants to stay relevant at the cutting edge must continuously relearn things, attend distance courses and update their CVs with certifications from various fields of competence, technology and systems.

The challenge lies in the fact that there is so much to learn but so little time to learn it, which will cause learning to grow shorter and more compact—and all the more digital. In other words: accessible to everyone, almost regardless where in the world that person is located. Every single human will have the possibility to study, in the exact way and pace that is most compatible with his or her individual learning capacity.

Built on similar reasoning, massive open online courses (MOOCs) and "mobile microlearning" were invented—the former for continuous learning and the latter for nugget-sized inspiration and knowledge that can be absorbed anytime, anyplace in the time it takes a person to use the bathroom. A kind of digital kaizen for digital talents, in its most modern versions with AI for personalization, utility tokens for economy and bullet proof blockhchain certification for credibility (read more on aiar.com).

Digital learning

And what exactly is it that we must learn?

In the fields of communication, digital marketing and sales is absolutely compulsory to know. For that exact reason, "DMP"—The world's 2nd biggest – application for digital marketing and sales—was born (find it at App Store and Google Play). Knowledge of social media, search strategy, digital campaigns, site optimization, digital CRM—these are all vital ingredients in a digital strategy. But of course, this you already know!

But who is the person that nods her head at each of the previously mentioned Re-cepies for Digital Re-cruitment; continuously learns new things; performs digital trendspottings; and constantly certifies herself in the newest digital communicative competence fields and methodologies? Well, that person is the digital super talent and winner of 2018 and onward. Whether we like it or not. Whether we see it as an "annoying problem" or an "inspiring challenge".

This is what is required of us to succeed.

After all, what is more inspiring than acquiring new knowledge? And what is more stimulating than using that knowledge to incite exciting changes?

Summary

It is getting more obvious that the digital revolution is entering its third phase. The digital now permeates entire populations, industries and countries. This shift is generally referred to as the Digital Transformation.

Whether we are talking about the evolution of the internet itself, connectivity or hardware, digital *communication* technology has played a central role in the development of the digital revolution. Research claims that this revolution is instigated by a highly social process, and *consumption* plays at least at big role – where communication has gone from monologs to dialogs, where we have progressed from nonlinear company communication to nonlinear consumer behavior, and where the majority of today's activities and campaigns are digital. The third force is the *commercial*, where a huge array of companies want to bridge the gap between communication technology and what the freedom-thirsting consumers want.

The digital revolution has brought about major consequences for many people, societies and countries. The digital contributes to an ever-growing portion of *countries'* GDPs, a trend which is not likely to change. Ventures that naturally adapt to the new digital world challenges basically all aspects and *companies* of traditional markets with new, revolutionizing technology, digital distribution and innovative business models. These new companies are usually very aware of the need for an elastic and flexible organization, the value of using digital technology and processes, and the importance of recoding the company's very DNA to incorporate the digital.

Individual people are faced with a growing list of necessary digital qualifications, such as "the 10 Re-cepies for Digital Re-cruitment". Lifelong learning has become completely vital to staying relevant on today's job market, and new inventions such as MOOCs and microlearning are necessary tools on the way to becoming the digital superhero.

CHAPTER 6: THE LARGEST EMPIRE THIS WORLD HAS EVER KNOWN

What will we learn? *The latest digital megatrends.*
Why is this important? *To arm ourselves against the future, and emerge as winners once it is upon us.*

Forget the legacy empires left behind by Alexander the Great and Genghis Khan. Even the British Empire has no say in this matter. The largest empire in the history of mankind is without a doubt the digital. It is virtually a no-man's-land, but its size dwarfs any physical realm. Yet we are steadily approaching a point where *everything* is hooked up to this massive digital realm, and unlike our "real" world, the cyberworld is highly malleable and dynamic. Things happen with such blinding speed that our only hope of future-proofing lies in keeping an unwavering weather eye on all the things happening in *both* these worlds.

This is unfortunately not something we can just do once and then be done with. Just like the world we mean to chronicle, this is an ongoing process; we must keep constant track of the events to have any hope of staying relevant in our digital marketing efforts—and really everything else as well.

In line with this need of keeping "constant track", we in this chapter offer some of the most crucial "digital megatrends" for you as a marketer 2018 and onwards. Having said that, some of the content in this chapter is the kind of stuff we will "laugh" at tomorrow, because a content of the trendspotting for this year will quite unavoidably be outdated in the same amount of time. Still, if we forget the content and look at the highlevel patterns, there are som signs that *will* become the predominant flavor of the world ahead. And from a *consumer perspective* these patterns are spelled 5 digital megatrends, starting with digital commerce, mobile devices, social as well as animated communication and, most of all, data. All from a *corporate perspective* boiling down to 3 strategic outlines for digital power and ultimate success.

The digital megatrends shaping our world

As artificial intelligence is relentlessly approaching its tipping point with the speed of light, automation is going to have profound implications for people and their jobs. Meanwhile, the world is in turmoil as there are currently over 66 million forcibly displaced people across the globe—more than half% of whom are children. Wars and bloody conflicts by the score keep raging, and already limited resources grow scarcer by the day. Medicinal breakthroughs help us live longer and the global birth rate is twice as large as the death rate—Earth is overpopulated to the degree of bursting at the seams, and there is no sign that the growth is waning.

All these things are but mere glimpses into the earthshaking forces at play around us, and from the eye of the storm rises the digital to eclipse it all. Because amid all the colossal powers at play, the digital must surely be the largest and most awe-inspiring. The digital tsunami that is flushing across the face of the planet is unlike anything we have previously witnessed, and it will leave nothing untouched.

As of 2016, the digitalization is no longer exclusively confined to First World countries—it is going on everywhere. In the world of business, it isn't just marketing that is experiencing turbulence—everything is either in the process of or soon to be reformed. For individuals everywhere, the digital is becoming a more and more self-evident part of their lives, and to an extent that is growing by the day, the digital is spreading to even babies and older people.

It has gotten to the point where it is no longer considered a conspiracy theory to say that the digital is taking over the world—it is now common knowledge. Whether people have given it enough thought or not, they subconsciously know it is happening. If you were a particularly daring futurist some 25 years ago you could have read the signs and trends and see where we were headed, but who would have believed you? Today? Who would even be surprised?

Digital business in a league of its own
Our first digital megatrend could just as well be called The Grand Crusade of E/M-Commerce. And with titans such as Alibaba, Amazon and eBay supplying everyone with the ability to buy anything, anytime, anywhere; and App Store and Google Play raking in yearly revenues in the double-digit billion-dollar range, it's not hard to see why.

While petroleum and pharmaceutical company take-overs are still taking technological ones to school, Zuckerberg's 2014 $19 billion purchase of WhatsApp, Dell's 2015 $66 billion merger with data storage company EMC, and Microsoft's 2016 $28 billion acquisition of LinkedIn give a nod as to how valuable the digital goods have become. Zuckerberg was even quoted saying '$19 billion for WhatsApp is cheap'!

A mobile super-highway to the future
The second digital megatrend is already well on its way to taking over the world. Mobile multitasking is growing more prevalent by the minute; people access the phone *everywhere*—even while consuming other media, such as TV, cinema and games. "Second screen" is a phenomenon that is here to stay… and *grow*.

And there is a reason for that. Unlike stationary and laptop computers, the mobile phone is a truly global accessory. Having your own PC is by no means a privilege reserved for every human, but the number of worldwide mobile phone users is now passing 5 billion. With a global population of 7.5 billion people, that's no mean feat.

Regardless the device, mobile has rooted itself firmly at the heart of our digital expansion, and a glimpse at the horizon suggests that we will be privy to a lot more excitement in this area. Everyone wants to be constantly connected to the mobile world, and our beloved phones is the first step to truly realizing that dream. Wearables like Fitbit and Apple Watch and even the flopped Google "Glassholes" can also be seen as steps toward a similar digital utopia, the hype of the HoloLens and Magic Leap even more. But none of that matters. When virtual reality (VR)—and much, much more importantly augmented reality (AR)—passes the point where it is no longer just a fun thing to have for the tech-savvy enthusiast, mobile will *truly* flex its muscles. AR-glasses is one thing. Soon we will be wearing digital lenses controlled by eye-tracking, and soon thereafter surgically installed, neuron-controlled digital retinas.

The mixed realities, in which we will seamlessly zap back and forth between a ***Real***, an ***Augmented*** and a ***Virtual*** reality, will grow to become almost inseparable features of our lives to the point where we will literally experience withdrawal symptoms in their absence. AR (VR is unfortunately a little too "stationary" to truly take over the world) will be such an indescribably critical constituent of the digital future that one could quite effortlessly write a book about or launch an app on that subject alone. If you find AR as interesting as me, a comprehensive free-to-download trendspotting white paper on that topic—and several others of equal importance to the future—has been published at www.aiar.com/trendspotting.

A new generation of social relations

The third digital megatrend—social media and digital social relations—is fusing with almost everything on the web worth mentioning. Retail. News. PR. Gaming. Dating. Just to name a few. Among these, the latter has truly experienced an upswing unlike any other. Tinder is hellbent on giving the world a new meaning of the word promiscuity, and with over 26 million matches—*every day*—they are doing a pretty good job.

In the somewhat more political sphere, the latest report shows that the chat application WeChat has 963 million users worldwide—nearly 500 million of whom are from China, despite the infamous censorship of the Chinese version of the app. In other news, there are now 2 billion Facebook accounts, with five new ones created every second.

In the true spirit of P2P sharing economy, Airbnb and Uber guides the way by enabling microentrepreneurs all over the world—more specifically, in 191 and 83 countries respectively. With the latter allegedly valued at around $70 billion, it is success beyond what any taxi company has ever dared dream of.

But this is also the time of P2P regulations meant to inhibit such private transactions. Meanwhile, the usage of Adblockers and VPNs has never been higher.

Bottom line is, these days everything is about digital relations; everywhere, all the time. At the same time, these relations are engaged in a bloody freedom war to stay social and uncontrolled; yet with our totalitarian dependence on the American platforms, the filter bubbles derive us of oxygen and we are being suffocated by their omnipresence.

Video media rising

The fourth digital megatrend is video media, and video media is taking the world by storm. This is a time when blogging is yesterday's news and vlogging is the new black; when selfies are going out of fashion and videoselfies and vidfies are the only ways to stay hip; and when user-generated content looks so high-end that it is often mistaken for editorial content. And for the latter reason it is also the time when fake news is so ubiquitous that it has even become a mudslinging weapon in presidential elections.

This is a time when making a living as a YouTuber is common practice, as clearly evidenced by the prime example PewDiePie, whose channel is presently over 16,000,000,000 views strong and whose multimillion earnings have attracted both the attention of Forbes and Guinness.

It is a time when companies with the right business concept, such as Netflix, rakes in $5.5 billion in revenue from over 80 million paying users; a time when linear TV is being phased out by digital VOD and online content.

This is a time when silent text and dead imagery has nothing to show for anymore, while vivid audio-and-video communication totally dominates.

Data – the heart of the digital ecosystem

AR may very well be the face of the future, but the mastermind behind everything will be data. Our worlds will be utterly personalized by hyperintelligent AIs in combination with the virtual zettabytes of digital data left behind by the inhabitants of an internet that will soon permeate almost every aspect of our lives. That which was once about atoms and molecules is now so much more about ones and zeroes.

Computational power has since long reached the point where it can efficiently decipher digital big data; the Internet of Things (IoT) is expanding its virtual kingdom on an almost daily basis; and as a result, increasingly smart applications are interconnected machine-to-machine (M2M) in ways we have never seen before.

But what's the deal with data anyway? Well, the deal is that our individual annual digital footprints range well above

1 terabyte now. Does that sound like a lot? Or not? Let me put it this way: if all these ones and zeroes were arranged next to each other in a long line, it would not take us from Paris to Madrid, not from Europe to America, not around the globe. It wouldn't take us to the moon, nor to Mars, nor to Jupiter. It would take us to Saturn and back. 25 times. This is the incomprehensible amount of data that a *single* person leaves behind. Every year.

All this data is now being used practically through e.g. big data for advanced analysis and insights. It will also provide the foundation for AIs to learn, adapt and contextualize, which will not only further AI dramatically, but also aid companies to realize their potential and make lives easier and better for individual people.

And as the interconnection between machines takes off, predictions for the future emerge en masse. Fifty billion machines connected to each other by year 2020? Sure, but no matter how crazy that may seem in the presence, such prophecies tend to ultimately be underestimations. Take drones for instance. The Federal Aviation Administration originally predicted that 15,000 of them would be out and about by 2020. That forecast was slightly off; by 2016 there had already been 2.5 million sales. PWC has since predicted the market to be worth $127 billion by 2020. Quite the revision indeed. And considering how indescribably large the field of application for digital data is, it is at least not crazy to assume that most predictions are actually lowballing the future.

A new era of digital power

The digital realm *is* a no-man's-land… but that doesn't mean people aren't trying to claim it. More and more gorillas are emerging from the djungle, trying to stake their claims on a brave new world filled with promises of power and money.

At the time of writing, Amazon is increasing its sales YOY

by unbelievable 34%, resulting in Bezos superseding Gates… as the world's richest man. That's 18 years on the throne, if you were wondering. Meanwhile, Alphabet, with its flagship product Google, increases its revenue with 24% YOY, with a 2017 Q3 revenue of $27 billion. Alibaba, Apple, Airbnb. And of course Facebook. They are all leading the way into the digital world. Of the five highest valued brands in the world, four are now digital (Google, Facebook, Microsoft and Apple). A closer look tells us that six of the ten richest people in US have amassed their fortunes by way of the digital, and in record-time at that.

I'm talking about Bezos, Zuckerberg, Brin, Page, Gates… they all get it. Some more than others.. While the "digital dinosaurs" – of respect not outing them here – *don't* get it. With a better understanding of the future are Apple, Microsoft with its Azure, Samsung with Galaxy and Bixby. They're in the game, they deliver, they're dabbling in AI. But they're no more than "digital dinorillas" at best. But then there are the "digital gorillas" – 800-pound beasts with AI encoded into their very DNA. Amazon, Alphabet, Alibaba, WeChat, Facebook. These guys are long past the unicorn stage (valuation of >$1 billion) and they trade more in power than money. They are the digital gorillas. *The* digital gorillas.

Three trends of global digital dominance

Above we have looked from a consumer perspective and found 5 digital megatrends, including digital commerce, mobile devices, social as well as animated communication and data. From a corporate perspective this is boiling down to 3 strategic outlines for digital dominance and ultimate success, more specifically AR, Asia and AI.

AR supremacy

Sure, the mobile is one of the prime constituents of digital dominion—I mean, what else is new?—but get this: it will be yesterday's news in just a few years. AR is the next step of the mobile phone. Remember the smartphone paradigm shift? How we went from our beloved Stone-Age Nokias to having smartphones, practically overnight? Now there are more mobile devices than people in the world. The same kind of paradigm shift will happen in a few years to come, as AR glasses replace smartphones.

And this is kind of important. After all, why is Amazon so big? Well, 700 million *mobile* customers are a start. Why is Google increasing its revenue so much? Well, 25% from desktop helps of course, but with more than 50% from mobile, it just goes to show. And Zuckerberg's success, where did that come from? In terms of revenue, around the time when he *really* went mobile—and perhaps it was good that he did, since 87% of his income today comes from the mobile.

Asian supremacy

The most promising business comes from the mobile today, but if that is the tool, where in the world do we actually use it? Considering the fact that 54% of the global population resides in Asia (in contrast to Europe's 11% and North America's 5%), that *might* be a good place to start. If we then take into account the record-high internet penetration—50% of the global population—we're getting closer to the answer. Add to that the fact that Asia has the world's highest mobile penetration, and it doesn't exactly take a large leap of the imagination to understand where I'm going with this.

The Chinese BAT companies (Baidu, Alibaba and Tencent) are all challenging the three American AAA-companies (Alphabet, Amazon, Apple)in their respective online categories. It's small wonder that Amazon is investing heavily in the Asian market, with a logistical base in Singapore, a game plan to enter the tough Korean market and 5 billion invested dollars in the Indian market alone. And why exactly is that small wonder? Because Alibaba is coming for them. In terms of valuation, the latter is closing in on Amazon. With a 61% valuation increase Alibaba is steadily approaching the magical $500 billion market cap. Amazon has been given a run for its money, to be sure.

It doesn't really come as much of a surprise that Asia is Alphabet's biggest market (in headcounts) either. They are the biggest in all the Asian countries except China, where Baidu is still holding its own.

Myapp (Tencent) is cathing upp the App Stores with 25% coverage, with Apple the double while Alphabet a mere 5%. Zuckerberg too is flexing his muscles in Asia; Facebook has an awe-inspiring penetration everywhere in Asia, except in China where it is currently blocked (which only makes Facebook's 40% Asian penetration all the more amazing).

AI supremacy

Now we're approaching the secret sauce to success for 2018 and onward. To become a digital gorilla, the business ought to be conducted in Asia and the product ought to be (read *must be*) presented on the mobile phone today and AR-glasses tomorrow… but what *is* the product?

It should come as no surprise at this point that we're talking about AI. This is not the science fiction of tomorrow. Our three digital gorillas show that this is so—today! AI will quickly become the key to global supremacy, and in a disruptive process eerily akin to Darwinian survival-of-the-fittest, it will separate the winners from the losers. It doesn't matter if we're talking about "real AI" or machine learning. The nature of the beast is beyond the point—the point is the application of the technology. Hyper-personalized search engines? Programmatic media acquisitions? Personalized consumption? Everything—EVERYTHING—will be governed by AI.

And there we are approaching the ABC of the secret sauce 2018 and onwards. With **AI-applications** as the core product, all implemented in decentralized P2P-processes secured by **Blockchain technology**. And, eventually – in the 2nd wave after the netscapes, myspaces and altavistas we now see in the bit- and altcoins of the 1st wave – all paid for by the **Cryptocurrency** of utility.

But who will rule tomorrow?

You know it already. Google's top-ranked futurist predicted that the world's largest digital company by the year of 2030 will be a digital school. I am fully convinced that the next A to be added to this extensive list of digital A-gorillas (Apple, Alphabet, Amazon, Alibaba, Adobe, Azure, AirBnbetc.) will be AIAR (www.aiar.com). Specifically, the market will be that of learning—but not like it looks today. The market for learning is one of the biggest in the world, and it's just lying there, waiting for disruption. Well, it will be disrupted soon—by yours truly. AIAR will democratize and personalize learning, make it enjoyable and magical, and make it accessible to *everyone*, regardless where in the world that person is located. By the ABC of using *AI for personalized learning*, *Blockchain technology* for a global standard of secure certification, and *Cryptocurrency* with utility tokens for budgeting and planning of your lifelong learning. All, of course through the mobile today and AR-glasses tomorrow. Being born global with representation in 165 countries in general but with Asia as the predominant market in particular.

This is going to be the coolest journey in the history of mankind. Bar none.

Summary

In this chapter we have put five digital megatrends under the microscope and seen how both their individual powers, and more importantly, their collective synergism molds both our physical "real" world and our virtual digital world. These trends encompass things like record-high digital business as a highly potent incentive to further technology; mobile as an incontestably dominating channel and a highway conduit to true just-in-time access; social relations as a next evolutionary step after traditional interaction; video media and interactive content as the undisputed champion over their static and "dead" counterparts; and digital data as the ultra-potent engineer and enabler behind the scenes.

MODEL OF THE FIVE MEGATRENDS

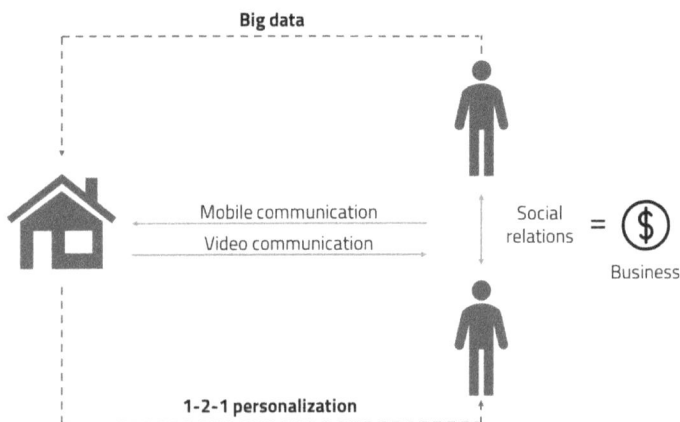

These trends translate to profound consequences for the entire world, and consequently also impact digital marketing and sales so much that without a good grasp of these forces, a digital marketer would never even stand a chance in the long run. The extreme repercussions for the business-part of DMS; the mobile explosion within all five digital marketing means; the complete transformation of social media content and context strategy; virality, video media and mobile apps' proud ascension to the winners' stand of information and content; and the dominion of digital data and the hyper-accurate targeting and supreme communicative personalization it permits. These forces have the power to move mountains— or shape worlds.

A new era is dawning, and endowed with our digital strategies we will enter it as winners. By incorporating the consequences of these five digital trends we will also live on as such. Adding to this the three strategic outlines för power and dominance will shape the world once and for all, with the AR shaping the perception, with Asia changing the direction, and AI changing the actual reflection. For everything. For exactly everything.

CHAPTER 7:
THE SELF-CONSCIOUS E-PILOG

What will we learn? *What will come to revolutionize tomorrow's digital marketing and sales.*
Why is this important? *To survive the coming of the future; to rule it; and to really make a difference.*

When boys become bots and man becomes machine

And so—we are now the proud owners of a digital strategy, complete with digital scorecards and a made-to-order organization armed to the teeth with everything it needs to take on the new disruptive digital technology. With a fresh trendspotting in our pocket, we are now ready to assume the title of tomorrow's digital heroes. Now there is only one item left on the agenda.

But to be honest, this epilog is not to bid all you dear readers goodbye; I needed an excuse to talk about one of the coolest events to unfold since... let's say 1950 😉. Forget all the hypes. Forget wearables, AR, retargeting, 3D printers, Kurzweilian implants and the rest of the allegedly greatest things since sliced bread.

The singularly most important thing to befall this world since the advent of the steam engine and electricity—and perhaps the conception of ARPANET—is the fact that for a few years now, humans are interchangeable with machines.

This started when Eugene Goostman, a 13-year-old boy/ bot with a seriously quirky personality, passed the Turing Test. The media circus that followed was hardly unexpected, and while fans and skeptics bandied acclaim and criticism between them, the fact was that the bot fooled 30% of the judges—which incidentally is the criterion for passing the test. At the time of writing, this was three years ago. Do you think the AI race ended there?

The more recent capital-lettered proof that AI is about to hit the knee of the curve is called DeepMind. In March of 2016, one of DeepMind's tendrils AlphaGo defeated the eighteen-fold world champion Lee Sedol in Seoul with 4-1—a feat AI connoisseurs believed would take about a decade more. The truly astonishing thing about DeepMind itself is the fact that its intelligence is not preprogrammed; it does not secure knowledge and learning deductively, but *in*ductively… perhaps even abductively. For that reason, DeepMind theoretically has the potential to go toe-to-toe with anything… previously a privilege solely reserved for the diversity of human intelligence, now on the verge of becoming superintelligence

All of this is pivotal for every single one of Mother Earth's inhabitants, but for us working in the digital world it is flat-out profound. The digital tsunami is coming for all of us, and although that sounds almost ridiculously melodramatic, it is no less true

And so the question left for us to ponder is: will humanity finally reach the point where it is outmaneuvered by a new apex predator-in-the-making? Take for instance bitter-toned studies like "Race Against the Machine", where machines are shown to steadily approach the point where they—among *many* other things—irreversibly transform employment as we know it. A little more straight to the point: are machines taking over? Are they becoming so human that they will actually take our place? Are they becoming so human… that they will even gain awareness?

What does this have to do with digital strategy?

Imagine an intelligent machine that absorbs all the data our monumental digital footprints leave behind. Now imagine if that computer could process this data in real-time, learn from it and then also act on it. And, preferably, in as human a way as possible.

This stuff was already going on in 2015. The year when bot quite rightfully became a buzzword.

Now consider how prevalent digital relations are today. Consider how SMSing is quickly fading as a means to connect, while mobile chat apps like FB Messenger, Skype, WeChat, Snapchat, and Whatsapp are dominating the social communication between humans.

Some 84% of mobile internet users would use a chat app if one of their friends used it, and for 65% it already is the highest prioritized channel for communicating with friends and family.

But we're not talking Siri or Digby here. Teach an (artificially) intelligent bot the abstract rules of such digisocial behavior and we will see what digital marketing *really* is. We will have bots that quite effectively personify companies. The days when consumers must search far and wide for the products they like are over—they will just ask the bot. Forget queuing for service—just ask the bot. No more scanning sites or papers for news—just ask the bot. Few are the things that are more important for branding and business than what the "company" (read *the bot*) actually says, how it is said, how easy it is to understand, what tone it is said in… how *personalized* the communication is.

By all appearances, it could just as well be the company marketing director—why, even the CEO himself—serving millions of end consumers simultaneously. *Mass-customization* replaces *Mass-communication*, and the resulting 1-2-1 dialogs rise to an unprecedented level. This is DMS of the highest order. AI will become the new cornerstone of everything that marketing and sales is.

And all of it based on a bot that is truly "human"... perhaps even so human that it/he/she has an actual consciousness?

The mysterious allure of conscious machines

Because the keyword in these discussions is really that: consciousness. Isn't it a beautiful word? A truly *human* word? A word around which innumerable philosophical discussions have revolved. A root problem is that no one knows how to define consciousness from an objective, third-person perspective—we only ever have access to our own consciousness—and as such we don't know much about animal minds, and whether they are conscious or not. What about fish? Insects? Bacteria? Trees? Stones? How about machines?

Well, we know what Peter Singer would have answered, what with his distinction between sentience and self-consciousness (being conscious with the ability to feel pain and pleasure, and therefore have interests in being treated in particular ways, as opposed to being aware of one's self)—the latter of which he only attributes to humans and a small number of animal species (but not rocks).

But can machines really do the things we do?

Naturally, I dropped this question on FB. One of my martial art peers immediately asked whether a machine could be spontaneously sarcastic.

Well, if a sense of humor was the ultimate litmus test, I daresaythat machines can have consciousnesses. At the very least, I know how I would go about outlining an AI for a bot whose purpose it would be to use questionable humor to amuse nerds—and perhaps even others of a more "sophisticated" disposition. If anyone is willing to take that bet, I will be more than happy to present the proof.

Be that as it may, a sense of humor, sarcastic or otherwise, is unfortunately not intrinsic evidence of consciousness, even though many would argue it is a quality exclusively native to the human domain. Another such area where it is claimed that machines have nothing to show for is proactivity (often stated with something along the lines of "and thank God for that"), where the bot—like many animals—will only respond to certain stimuli which either we or nature feeds to it. "Unfortunately", I have tons of evidence where digital bots parade that very trait.

A closely related quality is the ability to ask relevant questions—something both Socrates and I argue to be even more important than Answers. This is also an area where the most sophisticated AI bots prevail, by devouring data and then asking relevant questions either as a result or in order to gain more information.

Whichever the case, it generally boils down to two things. The first one is to know enough digital psychology to understand how a human "would have" acted (or, in more practical terms, how "a number of different types of intentions in a number of different types of contexts makes a number of different people inclined to act in regard to a number of different types of questions").

The second one is to be digistrategic enough to be able to abstract the many different scenarios that might eventuate in response to a human being's actions, as well as derive how other people would game-theoretically respond to that action with respect to the social interaction between people in that very specific context.

But can machines really feel the things we feel?

Another friend—this time from the world of theater—roots his argument in more artistic light. He maintains that consciousness is something we "feel" through contact and presence, in much the same way a performer might feel a connection with both co-performers and the audience… and perhaps a little in the way a person doesn't have any problems separating a sleeping human from a corpse.

And if the litmus test goes along these lines instead… well, then things are different. Now we are talking about feelings—that is, nothing that must be proven or explained—but *shown*, *felt* and *understood*.

Many a doctor has praised the laying-on-of-hands act as fundamental in both diagnostics and remedies, and that is no religious fancy by any means. Things of such nature create a sense of consciousness in the patient, which some argue can never be replicated digitally on a distance or by a bot.

At the same time, I have met some of the world's most prominent doctors—global experts in their fields—who have very successfully performed advanced long-distance diagnoses and prognoses digitally to large numbers of people.

And if we leave the body behind in lieu of the soul, we reach another human need: *love*. The dominion of digital dating has its fair share to say on the subject. Hundreds of millions of people are busy online-dating every day, and are—to various degrees of course, and depending on their generation—perfectly happy with that. Unsurprisingly, there have been tests in which machines have dated humans online, and even had modest success in some cases. And there's definitely more where that came from.

Another very basic human need is *friendship*. Billions of people every day are content with communicating and nurturing relationships via posts, inboxes, emails, Skype calls, chats, snaps, tweets, pics and clips. Yet again, there are here machines (apps) for us to communicate with, and the result is not as far from human as one would think. Be that as it may, when two computers unwittingly interact with each other, any witness is in for a good time, as such M2M encounters have been known to spawn some pretty hilarious dialogs.

Yet experiments have clearly demonstrated that these machines *can* influence human feelings and even emotions, and strongly too. And again, there's going to be plenty more where that came from.

Moving on from our private lives to our *working lives*, the Alexandrian cut in mass communication occurred when we started using advanced digital technology to accomplish behavioral targeting that individualized the message so successfully that it virtually became 1-2-1 marketing. In other words: *Machine-2-Man*. While this is an unparalleled victory for companies (no more shotgun shooting), individuals benefit equally in the sense that they no longer get spammed with irrelevant communication.

The point of all this is that irrespective whether we are talking about digital social communication between doctors and patients, companies and consumers, humans aching for a bit of love or friends trying to keep in touch, we have taken the first steps. These things *can* be digitalized without compromising the quality or value. What's more, as soon as it is digitalized, it can—both in theory and often in practice—be communicated by machines with artificial intelligence. Machines that can seemingly mimic consciousness with eerie precision— or perhaps, in the true meaning of the word, even attain such. It all seems to hinge on the question: what is consciousness?

Cogito ergo sum?

So, what is consciousness? A typical Cartesian treatise on dualism might dissect the question into the interaction between subject and object.

It is said that to *do* something consciously you have also reflected on why you are doing it, mapped out alternatives, evaluated them and then based the decision on a highly conscious consideration, which—if you also act on that consideration—becomes the "conscious action". Contrarily, something can be done unconsciously (in which case you would not know *why* you did it) or subconsciously (in which case you would not even know *that* you did it).

In turn, it is said by some that to *be* conscious is to take conscious decisions and carry out conscious actions—i.e. to not instinctively go from stimulus to response before taking that highly important route betwixt where a conscious consideration asks what the stimulus is and what the consequences of the response might be. Others maintain that being conscious is having the mental proficiency to perceive one's own presence in the surrounding world—in other words, having a subjective experience.

By this line of reasoning we can conclude that, if being conscious is contingent on carrying out conscious actions, stones are not conscious. But a digital bot can easily be programmed to take conscious decisions, and can—if uploaded to a ro-bot—even *perform* these conscious decisions. Eugene + exoskeleton = eMan.

But if our line of reasoning instead dictates that consciousness is having subjective experiences, to "sense" things, to "experience" the aroma of a certain flower or a woman, to "feel" certain feelings in response to e.g. success at work? Well, in that case emotions are constructed from physical things such as hormones and are thus quantifiable. We can program dopamine to release during the journey and serotonin to release at the end of it. Based on chaos theory and fractals we can—just like gods—design different "personalities", causing different bots to respond differently to the emotions generated by the same stimuli, thus creating highly "subjective" experiences.

So why could a consciousness like this not be developed and uploaded to locally exist within the scope of a machine? Or, even better, into an actual robot, which could then be used for all the "human" facets of life. Facets we have already started digitalizing, such as interaction with patients, consumers, clients, love and friends?

Why would anyone want conscious machines?

Perhaps the question isn't so much whether we *can* develop a machine with a consciousness, as *why* we would do it? Isn't humanity already overpopulated enough as it is, without the emergence of a new super-intelligent, highly conscious "species"? Why would we *consciously* create another contender for the space on a planet whose resources are limited, even as our population is already growing larger and older? If our filter bubbles already cause us to regress in terms of consciousness, shouldn't we try to nurture it and *develop* as human beings instead of allowing the digital inflation to phase our humanity out?

Perhaps, but—notwithstanding the fact that a digital future is unavoidable at this point—there are strong incentives for us to embrace digitalization. If there weren't, we would not be going in that direction at all. In our quest to give birth to machines with consciousnesses, there are three such incentives that are particularly salient:

First our almost spiritual desire for *love*. Imagine how many people in this world are lonely. Billions of them, to be sure. There are likely more of them in the Western world than in regions where the social is still considered the glue that keeps society, families and networks together. Some get a feline or canine companion to keep them company; others fill the emptiness with television, radio, mobile phone games or similar digital "buddies". For these people, the bot would constitute something as loyal as a dog, but also interactive and social—and perhaps even as intelligent and conscious as a human being.

Second our historical hunt for *assistance*. Subjects and slaves back then; paid aid today; and—maybe—bots tomorrow. Unlike our contemporary Lutheran era, both my friends Plato and Aristotle considered "work" to be something inhuman, even degrading. In their ideal, work was something solely reserved for slaves. And if it just "took care of itself", well then that would have been even better. Perhaps what they were after was bots? And actually, ever since the time of another one of my friends—Leonardo da Vinci—visionaries have been hard at work to create robots. The pursuit of automatization was revolutionized during the Industrial Age when the steam engine was invented; but the real breakthrough—at least if you were to ask Plato, Aristotle or da Vinci—occurred during the Information Age when industrial robots automated much of the laborious work previously done by humans. And now? With the Interaction Age in its prime and an estimated 50 billion connected machines by the year of 2020, people languishing for a more simplified life will have the time of their lives.There was even a time when slaves were not considered sentient "beings". Likewise, now is the time when many consider machines incapable of being conscious (or, that was how it was until they met the robot Sophia, and she got her citizenship in Saudiarabia cleared). Who's to say there won't come a time when we consider throwing out a computer murder? Maybe "android apartheid" is taking it too far, but it might be prudent to remember that the word robot derives from the Proto-Slavic word *orbota*, which means hard work… or slavery. Food for thought today, but moral ambiguity tomorrow?

Finally, we have humanity's strongest driving force—well, at least according to the Maslow Hierarchy of Needs. Self-actualization. Also known as existential angst. Why are we here? Is there meaning to life? And if there really is a meaning, why do we die? Is *immortalization* the answer we are looking for? It has surely been a recurring theme over the ages, with the construction of monuments, the writing of books, the composing of music, the victory of wars, the founding of companies, the winning of competitions, the acquisition of celebrity, even procreation itself. In a way, these are but pursuits of immortality in many different guises.

But imagine if you could actually create so conscious a synthetic clone of yourself that it could be both a friend while you live, as well as a soulmate to your children and family when you die? Because what exactly is it that "disappears" when we die? Is it the allegedly 21-gram "soul"? Nope, modern science debunked that myth a long time ago. Is it just our body? Maybe, but then the issue of a bot's consciousness becomes even more banal. Or is it what we call "consciousness" that disappears? And in that case, is it possible a bot could actually "take over" that consciousness? Could we upload our mind or soul or consciousness—it's just different words for the same things—to a bot not shackled by the fragility of our flesh bodies? The keen pursuit of real androids is an example of such a driving force. And the keen pursuit of real androids post-Turing Test is extremely close to success.

Why *wouldn't* anyone want conscious machines?

It seems that the matrix isn't that far away. The opposing question—i.e. why would people *not* want conscious machines?—is therefore at least as relevant.

It doesn't take a digital guru to see that a conscious bot is a two-way street. Of course there might be both good and evil here. But guns don't kill people, people do. The gun isn't intrinsically evil. You can kill someone with a hammer too, but you can also build a castle or a hospital. It's all a matter of application—how the tool is used.

The Second Machine Age poses the argument that our jobs will disappear. A more apocalyptic take on the question concerns not only the matter of superintelligence through general AI, but the moment when machine becomes humanWhen it grows aware of its own existence. When it becomes concerned with its own existence. When it becomes protective of its own existence. And when it perhaps even starts seeing *our* existence as a threat.

But looking at things from a slightly more positive perspective—and I have personally never understood any other—I would be a liar if I said I didn't want to create one. Not because of the first reason though; I consider friends and family so infinitely more gratifying than the digital "flight from freedom" – as provided by gaming, TV and other types of digital entertainment. The desirous smell of a woman, the silent excitement of climbing, the profound serenity of diving, the adrenaline-fueled action of boxing, the intellectual stimulation of discussing life and philosophy with friends, the contentment of seeing a child's contagious smile light up its entire face. These are all things I still prefer live, so to speak.

The second reason is not the one either. I can "hold my own" in this regard. More importantly though, digital assistance has the tendency to cause harm even as it helps. Google makes our memories worse; calculators make us bad at counting; platforms limit our perspectives with their filter bubbles. We are getting more handicapped and weak as we rely more and more on machines, and meanwhile the machines are growing stronger and smarter. With digital crutches, we are slowly forgetting how to walk. internet is changing our minds and formatting our brains in an eerily literal sense.

No, it is actually the third reason that drives me—immortality. And I don't mean "feeling" immortal, which I do all the time (as a rock climber, martial artist, 16h-working serial entrepreneur, adventurer and volunteer I am frequently accused of behaving as such). What I mean (obviously) is becoming immortal "for real", and in the future (equally obviously) constructing my own bot, a bot whose name would (even more obviously) be Rubot.

So, if you scare easily, perhaps now is the time to look away. Because I am definitely the kind of guy who could and would do something like this. I have the necessary digital tools; the necessary resources; and the necessary knowledge in terms of digital psychology and algorithms to orchestrate it. Most importantly though, I am "eccentric" enough (others would name it crazy) to actually go through with it.

It's just that… I don't have time to do it! Although if I did have a bot I *would* in fact have more time. But… starting to sound like Epimenides paradox? I think I need a smart buddy—Rubot—to brainstorm with. Let me get back to you on it all.

Last but not least:
a big THANK YOU

If you have been reading this book non-stop during a coffee break you might get surprised. This book was NOT written during a day. It has, in fact, been developed over a long period of time. It is the result of working together with respected corporations and having endless discussions with many intelligent individuals. Even if I take full responsibility for the content, it is the outcome of interactions with a wide range of wonderful people – some of them completely unaware of it.

Client wise, we will find world-leading corporations such as Samsung, Mercedes, IKEA, Electrolux, PWC, Schenker, Cap Gemini and many more. If we look to the organizations, we will from the early stages of digital times find the world organization of digital marketing, IAB. On the other side, in present time, we have the world's biggest advertising corporations, WFA.

On the entrepreneur side we have our oldies but goldies from pioneering businesses within AV-online and e-health.se as well as from a vast array of companies where my role has been as a partner or board member. Today we find stars from several other businesses such as mobile gaming, digital dating and medtech to mention a few.

On a personal side, some of these heroes have been Malin, Simon, Frida, Anna and Jannice. Malin has not only been the most supportive speaking partner, researcher and script editor of this book, she has also been running a big group of digital consultants in one of my start-ups, which is now sold and listed on the stock exchange.

Right now I am on one of the world's most exciting and groundbreaking journeys. Together with a brilliant team of masterminds and digital go-getters, I am introducing a game changing digital ecosystem for learning. A system that will for the first time in the world make online learning personalized and easy to budget with a 100% secure certification process. How? By using the latest and most innovative ABC-technologies within AI, blockchain, and cryptocurrency. And so far so good as we today are the second most downloaded app within Digital Marketing, with highest reviews on both App Store and Google Play. None of of this could have been done without the most marvellous management, my hardworking wingmating pm, and the rest of the team today, yesterday and on their way in. All of them guided by a board of notabilities with a vast international experience and a number of unicorns in their portfolio – not to forget Albert Öjermark, who is the best senior advisor and the smartest person I have had the privilege to get to know.

On the private side, I want to thank all my friends who still have the energy to be my friends, despite my 90-hour work weeks. I want to thank my family, my wonderful wife, my cool sister and my mother. But most of all I want to thank my twins, Zeus and Leon, for which I also dedicate this book. You are the most beautiful people I have ever met and you have given me the most beautiful gifts in life. Before you two were born I didn't know that this could be reality. You give me love, happiness and strength and I hope I will manage to give you at least as much back.

Rufus Lidman, April 2018

www.ingramcontent.com/pod-product-compliance
Lightning Source LLC
Chambersburg PA
CBHW042120190326
41519CB00031B/7559